A GUIDE TO RECEIVING SUPERNATU

SUPERNATURAL POWER ON EARTH

EMBRACING THE HOLY SPIRIT

MATT MORGAN

SUPERNATURAL
POWER ON EARTH
Published by: S. Matthew Morgan
Fellowship of Praise Church
PO BOX 381 • Clarksville OH 45113
fopchurch.net

This book or parts thereof may not be reproduced in any form, stored in a retrieval system, or transmitted in any form by any means — electronic, mechanical, photocopy, recording, Internet, or otherwise — without prior written permission of the publisher, except as provided by United States of America copyright law.

Scripture quotations from the following versions are taken from digital Bibles accessed via Biblehub.com. © 2004 - 2017 by Bible Hub, a production of the Online Parallel Bible Project:

New International Version (NIV). Copyright 1973, 1978, 1984, 2011. Digital text courtesy of Biblica.com. Used by permission.

King James Version (KJV), Text courtesy of BibleProtector.com, KING JAMES BIBLE: PURE CAMBRIDGE EDITION: DIGITAL ELECTRONIC TEXT. Used by permission.

Scripture quotations from the following versions were accessed via BibleGateway.com, a division of The Zondervan Corporation:

New King James Version®. Copyright © 1982 by Thomas Nelson. Used by permission. All rights reserved.

Amplified® Bible (AMP), Copyright © 2015 by The Lockman Foundation. Used by permission. www.Lockman.org

Amplified® Bible Classic (AMPC),
Copyright © 1954, 1958, 1962, 1964, 1965, 1987 by The Lockman Foundation. Used by permission.

New American Standard Bible® (NASB), Copyright © 1960, 1962, 1963, 1968, 1971, 1972, 1973, 1975, 1977, 1995 by The Lockman Foundation. Used by permission. www.Lockman.org

International Standard Version (ISV). Release 2.0, Build 2015.02.09. Copyright © 1995-2014 by ISV Foundation. ALL RIGHTS RESERVED INTERNATIONALLY. Used by permission of Davidson Press, LLC.

The Message (MSG). Copyright © 1993, 1994, 1995, 1996, 2000, 2001, 2002. Used by permission of NavPress Publishing Group.

The following resources were used in biblical word studies:
Brown-Driver-Briggs Hebrew and English Lexicon, Unabridged, Electronic Database. Copyright © 2002, 2003, 2006 by Biblesoft, Inc. All rights reserved. Used by permission. BibleSoft.com

HELPS Word Studies, Copyright © 1987, 2011 by Helps Ministries, Inc.

Strong's Expanded Exhaustive Concordance of the Bible, James Strong. Thomas Nelson Publishers. Used by permission.

Thayer's Greek Lexicon, Electronic Database. Copyright © 2002, 2003, 2006, 2011 by Biblesoft, Inc. All rights reserved. Used by permission. BibleSoft.com

Copyright © 2018 by Matthew Morgan
ISBN 978-0-692-13826-7
First Edition Printing: June, 2018
Printed in the United States of America

Cover design by Drew R. Maddox

TABLE OF CONTENTS

Acknowledgements 4

Preface 5

1 God's Near Presence 11

2 The Third Person 23

3 First Response 43

4 The Hidden Spirit 57

5 The Anointing 77

6 Identity 99

7 Knowledge, Wisdom, & Discernment 121

8 Faith, Healing, & Miracles 143

9 Tongues, Interpretation, & Prophecy 167

10 Perceiving the Spirit: Avoiding Blasphemy 197

11 Global Salvation 215

12 Progressive Revelation 227

13 Living by Conviction 241

14 Application 259

ACKNOWLEDGEMENTS

To Bob "Mr. Cincinnati" Smith: I am grateful for your prayerful and financial support of this project. You have made a dream come true. May God bring seed to the sower, and may you be blessed with things money can't buy.

To Carol Smith I am indebted. It has been a privilege to work with you on this project. You have inspired me, encouraged me, and corrected me along the way. We have questioned, critiqued, and created this manuscript for the glory of God. Thank you, your support and spiritual insight made this possible.

To my FOP staff: You are the greatest. Thank you for your patience and grace. You make me better than I am.

To Bobbi, the love of my life, my companion and best friend: You are living proof that God's favor is upon my life.

PREFACE

Have you ever wondered who or what the Holy Spirit is? What does He do and how does He speak? Are you afraid of the Holy Ghost? Is He a spooky or friendly ghost? How do you navigate the nebulous world of the supernatural?

These questions and more are in the minds of many. There has never been a time when people are more hungry for supernatural reality. A quick glance at the television guide will reveal the number of shows dedicated to the paranormal. So where do you look to find truth on this subject? God's Word is rich in content on the spiritual world.

Drawing from the resources of Scripture and practical experience, this book will provide solid answers for those dissatisfied with the idea that supernatural activity is not real, as well as those seeking truth in this realm. In these pages, you'll read about the greatest supernatural power on Earth—the Holy Spirit. Practical, real-life examples of His power in action are given; your faith to trust and partner with Him will grow as you perceive His activity on Earth.

As you observe how He intimately works in the lives of believers today, you'll understand how He wants to equip you with His power. After all, we live, move and have our being in Him. God's power on Earth is only released through the Spirit. Jesus is the revelation of the Father, but the Spirit is the application of the Father. The Spirit is what God is doing on Earth. He invites you to tap into His supernatural ability so *you* can live a powerful life!

The Spirit of God has made me; the breath of the Almighty gives me life.

JOB 33:4 NIV

DANCE WITH THE ONE WHO BROUGHT ME

As a "first book," I never imagined that the Holy Spirit would be my topic of choice. In fact, it wasn't. Many other themes seemed more suitable for me and my particular experience. To attempt to write about the third person of the Godhead left me feeling so incompetent and unqualified. But the Spirit has left such a profound, indelible imprint on my life, I cannot help but offer to Him what's first. As I studied, prayed and sought the will of God, I kept finding myself circling back again and again, only to realize I must "dance with the one who brought me here." As hard as I tried, I could never be released from the burden of the Spirit.

Much of this book was written between 3 and 6 A.M. In those early hours of the day, the Spirit would awaken me. Then He would convey doctrine through the Word with conviction garnered throughout years of walking with Him. Many of the principles I will share were taught as a child. Over the years, God has shown me His supernatural power on Earth revealed through the Holy Spirit time and again. I have come to know and rely upon this ever-present power of God. I hope you too will discover the near presence of God through inspiration and revelation. My desire is that your relationship with the Spirit grows stronger through a fresh encounter with the Holy Ghost Himself. Through the Spirit, God has made Himself available to all who desire His involvement.

In this book I will attempt to answer common questions concerning the Holy Spirit, like who He is, what He does, and how He does it. There is much confusion and about the Spirit today. Satan would have it no other way. Realizing the Holy Spirit's threat to the demonic kingdom helps us to understand why there is so much resistance and confusion concerning the third person of the Godhead. Misinformation and confusion is the ploy of Satan; these tend to become areas of deception. This demonic strategy has been effective in detouring good people away from the Spirit's love towards them. Satan hates the Spirit. The Spirit offers peace, joy, power, direction, and understanding. What's not to hate if you are Satan?

In a confusing, combative world, the Spirit is present truth. He desires to be intimately known by His people; He desperately desires recognition by us, receptivity from us, and relationship with us. Unlike those who follow false deities, we can know Him. He is a Promise, not an acquaintance, a Companion closer than your breath. The Spirit is more than a force or energy; He is the third person of the Godhead communicating with us. Divine, yet accessible.

MISCONCEPTIONS OF THE SPIRIT

Many spiritual leaders appear as if they're buffering when asked piercing questions regarding the Spirit. If we don't know Him, how can we claim Him? Belief must be broadcast. We cannot share what we blatantly ignore.

The image of the Holy Spirit outside of the church is often perceived as creepy and weird. Although some attendees may merit this observation, not all do and certainly, He does not. It is unwise to place all who claim the same thing into the same box. Because they may claim the same thing does not mean they believe the same thing. Belief is backed by behavior! As a pastor of a Spirit-filled church, I am juxtaposed between trying to get "feeling people" to think, and "thinking people" to feel.

Unlike the "navel gazers" of transcendental meditation or the New Agers who falsely claim enlightenment, the Spirit is not a novelty to be toyed with, or the figment of someone's overactive imagination. He is God. The Spirit can never be reduced to man's restraints or limitations. There is no reading of tealeaves, no magic eight ball or bag of secrets. Simply put, the Spirit is on assignment from God on your behalf.

In some circles, the Spirit is treated as if He were an ethereal force that randomly pops in and out of our lives, like a jack-in-the-box. We are subject to His whims, never knowing if He will scare or surprise us. Some have viewed Him as a cosmic Santa Claus passing out lollipops, while others see a tyrannical, vindictive enforcer that will whip the world into shape. So, who is He?

The Holy Spirit is an encourager, requested by Christ, sent by the Father. The word "encouragement" means more than a pep talk, or comforting words. To encourage means to impart courage, strength, motivation, and supernatural power. This definition confirms that He is more than positive feelings or words of affirmation. He is a powerful force, dedicated to your success, the demonstration of God's protection and power in and over you.

THE TREASURE AVAILABLE TO YOU

It is the glory of God to conceal a matter; to search out a matter is the glory of kings.

PROVERBS 25:2 NIV

Hundreds of tons of dirt are sifted through to get to one ounce of gold. In our search to discover more about the Spirit, you will find Him worth the effort. His majesty is often cloaked in mystery. I believe this is intentional. God uses this posture of "hiding" to separate those who truly desire more from the insincere or casual inquirer. The search itself is the prerequisite to unfold the glory rewarded to the seeker. Dig in and immerse yourself in all things "Spirit"—you will be the beneficiary.

Like the Laodicean church in Revelation, we are rich, yet poor; we are clothed, yet naked. We have great worldly treasure, but are empty of what makes life truly rich. All of the comforts and money in the world will never satisfy the innate hunger for relationship with God that He has placed inside us. To find the true riches, this generation must experience the real presence and power of God. We need a fresh revelation of God's Spirit.

History tells us that the early church father Thomas Aquinas once visited Pope Innocent II at his palace in Rome*. The Pope was surrounded by opulence. Looking over the treasury of the church, he was counting out a large mound of gold coins.

Hovering over the display of wealth he looks at the theologian Thomas Aquinas and glibly says, "The church can no longer say, 'Silver and gold have I none' [Acts 3:6]."

To this, Thomas Aquinas replies, "True holy father, neither can she say, 'Rise and walk.'" (*Source: Samuel A. Bent, *Familiar Short Sayings of Great Men*, Boston: Ticknor and Co., 1887.)

We can no longer settle for prestige devoid of power. The affluence that promised us comfort and fulfilment has left us empty and confused. We must experience the true power of God on Earth. Let not this generation say, "We are blessed with goods" while incomplete and deficient of the Treasure of the Spirit.

The Holy Spirit is our Guide: He navigates our life through places, stages, and phases. He reveals how broken we are while simultaneously putting us back together. He is order to our chaos and clarity to our confusion. He is our help and our hope. He is the pledge and the promise of God. He reproves and recovers. He is God's supernatural power on Earth. The Spirit says, "Come!"

Chapter 1

POWER ON
GOD'S NEAR PRESENCE

WHAT DO I BELIEVE ABOUT THE HOLY SPIRIT?

In the Apostles' Creed (a statement of Christian belief handed down from the church fathers), we are left with the simple statement, "I believe in the Holy Spirit." That's not a lot to go on. That's it? "I believe in the Holy Spirit?" This is voiced in mainline churches across the world every Sunday. Millions of believers gather every weekend, going through the motions, unaware of what they believe about the Holy Spirit. The question remains: What do I believe about the Holy Spirit?

> *The question remains: What do I believe about the Holy Spirit?*

The Nicene Creed, a statement of faith widely used in Christian liturgy, is even more vague concerning the Spirit. It offers definition in its profession of faith towards the Father, and towards the Son, but offers none towards the Spirit. It states, "and we believe in the Holy Spirit." There is no in-depth understanding of the Spirit in its rhetoric. I am not a critic of the creeds; I'm just stating the obvious. Hosea said, "people are destroyed for lack of knowledge."

Most early Christians did not have the privilege of education we have been afforded. Our generation has no excuse, as we have been given more information at our fingertips than at any previous time.

Daniel 12:4 says that at the end times knowledge would be increased. Today, you don't have to have a college degree or sit under a wise sage; all you need is a computer to study any topic in the world at the tip of your fingers. Even with great advancements in education and opportunities to access knowledge widely available, many rely on dated information that's been passed down by word of mouth.

Many modern-day believers have held to the position that the Holy Spirit is an impersonal spirit that moves at God's request. Without a true understanding of the Spirit, many become disenfranchised with the whole idea. Therefore, this is all the more reason we need to know what we believe concerning the Holy Spirit. It is imperative that we be well versed in our own beliefs concerning this mysterious third person of the Trinity.

SPIRIT IS PRESENCE

Where can I go from your Spirit? Where can I flee from your presence?

PSALM 139:7

The questions asked in the verse above are not asked to get an answer but to make a point. In Hebraic poetry, especially in the Psalms, "synonymous parallelism" is often used. In this literary device, a concept is repeated twice but uses different words, images, or symbols to express the same thought. The lines are "parallel" in that they're juxtaposed and share the same idea; the repetition of the second line or phrase is synonymous to what has been expressed in the first. In other words, the rhetorical questions in this quotation have the same answer, offering the same antidote.

In this verse, Spirit is capitalized for identification, letting us know that "Spirit" refers to the person of the Holy Spirit. Essentially, the words "Spirit" and "presence" are synonymous. The take away: Spirit is presence. The psalmist is expressing more than just the omnipresence of God; he is establishing the principle that God's presence is occupied by His Spirit! Wherever God's presence is, God's Spirit is. Spirit is presence! We walk closer and are nearer to His presence than we ever recognize. As the psalmist expressed, "Where can we go; where can we escape?" The Holy Spirit is more than a force, an energy, or an eye in the sky; He is where you are right now. Am I speaking spiritually, emotionally, or physically? The answer is "Yes!"; He is where you are right now! Spirit is presence.

> The words "Spirit" and "presence" are synonymous. The take away: Spirit is presence.

AWAKENED BY THE SPIRIT

In the late 1940's, a young minister and his family were visiting New York City. The skyscape of downtown Manhattan was drastically different from what we view today. Tall buildings were quickly being erected; however, technology had not caught up to the aggressive construction. Many buildings lacked the modern convenience of central air conditioning. This young family was spending the night in such a place. It was not uncommon to raise the large windows to allow the air to circulate, enjoying the breeze that comes from outdoors. On the thirteenth floor, the family call it a day, and nestle in for a good night's rest.

In the middle of the night, the mother is awakened, not in a natural sense but by a supernatural encounter. She is kindled by the Holy Spirit. As she awakes to consciousness, she becomes aware of her own voice speaking in another language, a heavenly language. This is not

> At a moment's notice, the Spirit gives sobriety and clarity to life's unexpected difficulties.

a dream or a linguistic exercise; this is the Holy Ghost expressing himself through an unknown tongue. As her eyes slowly open, she is startled to dimly see a child's figure standing on the outside of the 13th floor window ledge; supernaturally, she experiences peace instead of panic. She gently awakens her husband who fluidly slips into the dark without a sound and retrieves his firstborn daughter, who is standing over the ledge with her eyes closed in sleep. She is in imminent danger, a small step away from serious injury or death, but is mysteriously rescued.

The mother who had been soundly sleeping was awakened and informed by an outside source, a higher power. At a moment's notice, the Spirit gives sobriety and clarity to life's unexpected difficulties. A coincidence or strange happening might not be as bizarre as it appears at first glance: God through His Spirit is watching over us.

His eyes are on the ways of mortals; He sees their every step.

JOB 34:21 NIV

This story is especially profound to me; the little girl standing on the banister is my mother. Had the Holy Spirit not awakened my grandmother, my mother may have fallen to her death, and I would have never been born. I like to put it like this: "The Holy Ghost saved my life!"

EVER-PRESENT AND ALL-KNOWING

"Am I only a God nearby," declares the Lord, "and not a God far away? Who can hide in secret places so that I cannot see them?" declares the Lord. "Do not I fill heaven and earth?" declares the Lord.

JEREMIAH 23:23,24 NIV

God fills the earth through His Spirit. The Triune God is not only omnipresent, He is omniscient. This means He is everywhere, and He knows everything. This sobering facet of God's being is possible because of His Spirit. The Holy Spirit is the executing power and presence of God upon the earth. Through time and eternity, it is His guidance and direction that sustain and secure our destiny.

As the pilot said to the passengers over the loud speaker, "I have good news and bad news, the bad news is we are lost, the good news is, we are making excellent time." Thankfully, He doesn't leave us in this lost condition! The Holy Spirit has come to show us our state and guide us to a safe landing. He is the administrative agent of the Godhead. He is the ways and means committee. He is the CIA, and He is our GPS. He is in charge of coordination and calculations, but most importantly, He is God on Earth and He is accessible to us.

> *Most importantly, He is God on Earth, and He is accessible to us.*

The Spirit encourages us to live by design and not by default. He continually gives course correction to our wayward path. He is not optional, He is essential.

In short, the Holy Spirit is a Comforter, Counselor, Advocate, Protector, Teacher, Helper, Defender, and Intercessor. He empowers us, He inspires us, He stands by us, and He corrects us in love. He is what we need, and when we need it!

THE BREATH OF CREATION

By the word of the LORD the heavens were made, their starry host by the breath of His mouth.

PSALM 33:6 NIV

The Hebrew word for breath (*ruach*) means "Spirit." He is the wind, the breath, the Spirit of God. In the Creation account, we find that He hovers over the face of the waters and empowers the words God speaks, bringing life, light, and order out of chaos. (See Genesis 1:2-4.)

> Although He is God, and represents God, we are His mission and His assignment.

He is in the creative process of everything we call life and in everything that pertains to existence. He truly is our help, sent from above. Although He is God, and represents God, we are His mission and we are His assignment. How could anyone say no to Him? He reveals the Father, He reveals the Son, while restoring mankind.

He is everywhere, and He knows everything, He fills the earth… He fills the earth! There is not a place He is not, and there is no place He does not know. His near presence assures us that no distance can separate us from Him; no darkness can hide us from Him; no failure can keep us from Him. He is tenacious, persistent, and reliable. He will not and cannot let you down; that would defy His very nature.

In deserting you, He would be in denial of Himself. He cannot deny Himself (2 Timothy 2:13).

If I say, "Surely the darkness will overwhelm me, and the light around me will be night," even the darkness is not dark to You, and the night is as bright as the day. Darkness and light are alike to You.

PSALM 139:11,12 NIV

NO INTEREST, NO ENTRANCE

Though I've said a lot about who He is, I cannot stress enough how much we need Him. Many have allowed the mystique of the Spirit to prevent them from engaging with the person of the Spirit. I want to strongly caution against this mindset, which produces distance from God. God is unhappy with distance; He desires nearness. He enjoys friendship and kinship.

Come near to God and He will come near to you.

JAMES 4:8A NIV

We are designed to respond to His compelling call. I believe we have a homing mechanism, much like the salmon, who can migrate out to sea for several years, only to return to spawn in the same stream in which they were born. This homing species utilizes open water navigation and a keen sense of smell to

> *We are innately inspired to find our Source of origin.*

miraculously find their way home. They go back to their beginning and place of origin. We are also innately inspired to find our Source of origin.

We are continually summonsed by His presence. Romans 8 says that the earth groans, the Spirit groans, and we groan. This is a deep, inarticulate sound of despair or pain, as in the pangs of childbirth. The earth moans in the pains of labor as it waits for the full revealing of God's children, and to be freed from its bondage to decay (vv. 19-22). We groan as we wait for the redemption of our bodies and our manifestation as His sons (v. 23). The Spirit groans within us, pleading on our behalf in harmony with God's will, assuring that all things will work for us according to His purpose (vv. 26-28).

Maybe you have felt discouraged and groaned within yourself; this often results in our hearts experiencing coldness and reluctance to approach God. Walls are erected and boundaries are imposed for self-protection, but they actually become the prison bars that prevent abundant life. When we are inattentive to His advances, we do more than deny him; we ultimately reject Him. When we fail to respond to His subtle invitations, we violate the relationship that actually sustains life. We become our own adversary, limiting our own opportunities for growth and relationship.

> We cannot live outside of His presence.

We cannot live outside of His presence. We can make money, make promises, or even make babies, but we can't make peace or happiness. You may temporarily *survive* outside of Him, but you will *never thrive* outside of Him.

THE UNKNOWN, UNWANTED GOD

The Holy Spirit has been referred to by some as "the unknown God." Others have considered Him the unwanted God. We may *say* we want

Him, but our *actions* are the evidence. If we truly desire Him, He will be in our actions as well as our thoughts. We will search for Him on weekdays, not just Sundays. We may pursue Him in the morning or deep in the night. We will push back our plates when our natural hunger is replaced with a new hunger.

For the kingdom of God is not a matter of eating and drinking, but of righteousness, peace and joy in the Holy Spirit...

ROMANS 14:17 NIV

Even though we have been prone to neglect the Spirt, He has patiently waited for our communication and participation. Even when we hesitate, that nudge, that pondering, is His invitation to come.

To recap, if there is no interest, there is no entrance. Searching for God is an inherent instinct; choosing to avoid the Spirit is a decision. Human beings have an innate hunger for spiritual interaction, whether they know it or not.

RELUCTANCE EVENTUALLY BECOMES REJECTION

Rejection is the harvest of reluctance. The mystery of the Spirit can produce a spirit of reluctance. At least that's what happened to me. Although I was raised to know God, I found that not having full understanding of the Holy Spirit in my mind had morphed into doubt, which produces disillusionment and eventually leads to sin. A significant revelation occurred in my life when I understood that God is more concerned with my faith than my understanding. This book is an attempt to understand more, but make no mistake about it:

> God is more concerned with my faith than my understanding.

You can mentally know more than anyone else, but if you lack faith, you will live a life of discouragement and disappointment. Faith is key. Our own opinions can quickly become idols; we form them, just as ignorant men of old formed an image representing a god, naively placing their faith in something they created in their own image. Our opinions must not be formed, but reformed and transformed by the power of God's Spirit.

Do not be conformed to this world (this age), [fashioned after and adapted to its external, superficial customs], but be transformed (changed) by the [entire] renewal of your mind...

ROMANS 12:2A AMPC

For this to happen, we must set aside our reliance on self and surrender our entire being to the Holy Spirit's desire. In the words of Ralph Waldo Emerson, "The mind, once stretched by a new idea or experience, can never return to its original dimensions."

We need not pump the brakes just because the road is unfamiliar. If you listen to your spirt (internal witness), you will become more and more familiar with the gentle nudging of God's Spirit. The Holy Spirit is admonishing and guiding you even now. His ways are higher than our ways and His thoughts are higher than our comprehension. He is the near presence of Almighty God. He is God's supernatural power on earth.

PINING FOR HIM

On River Street in Savannah, Georgia, is a statue to memorialize youthful love. "The Waving Girl" is an emblem of unrequited love. Florence Martus was born in 1868, the daughter of Sergeant Martus who was stationed at Fort Pulaski. The impressionable young girl fell in love with a sailor who pledged his love and promised to return. She also pledged to wait for him, as long as it takes… So every time a ship would sail into the Port of Savannah, there was Florence, with her faithful collie, waving a sheet to welcome her love back home. She even waved by lantern at night. She was unrelenting. Her devoted collie, who is also memorialized, proved to be her only solace and life companion. According to the Georgia Historical Society (accessed September 7, 2017, http://georgiahistory.com/education-outreach/historical-markers/hidden-histories/the-waving-girl/), "Lonely sailors strained their eyes to look for her. They called her the 'sweetheart of seafaring men of the world.' She represented the wives and sweethearts they had left on distant shores. For others, it was her consistency that earned their fancy. During her forty-four years on the Island, Martus waived to an estimated 50,000 boats." She makes me sad, very sad.

> "Lonely sailors strained their eyes to look for her.... It was her consistency that earned their fancy."

The Holy Spirit comes by invitation, and stays by interest. If there is no interest, there is no entrance. Like Florence, the Spirit is unrelenting. Faithfully He intercepts, interrupts, and even invades, but it is up to us to entertain his advance. We may be found resembling the wayfaring sailor who never returned, who had an intention but no true interest.

Lord, help us not to be inconsistent in our fascination and fervor for you. May our eyes strain like those of the seafaring men looking for "The Waving Girl"; may He find us searching for Him with hearts of passion!

I wait for the Lord, my whole being waits, and in his word I put my hope. I wait for the Lord more than watchmen wait for the morning, more than watchmen wait for the morning. Israel, put your hope in the Lord, for with the Lord is unfailing love and with him is full redemption.

PSALM 130:5-7 NIV

Chapter 2

POWER ON
THE THIRD PERSON

THE PERSON OF THE HOLY SPIRIT

The Holy Spirit is not a what, but a who. He is not an it, He is the third person of the Godhead. He is a self-conscious, rational, individual person. A person has emotions, a will, and a purpose. He is not an energy or force. He is not an object that you can pick up or put down. He is alive and powerful. He lives on planet earth but prefers to live inside of you.

The Holy Spirt can be grieved, offended, pleased, or resisted. He can be honored or ignored. He can be quenched, lied to, or sinned against. And, in the worst-case scenario, He can be blasphemed.

> *Satan would love to create confusion around the Holy Spirit; after all, the Spirit leads us into salvation, which is ultimate deliverance from Satan.*

The personhood of the Holy Spirit has been a point of contention for many throughout the ages. Of course, Satan would love to create confusion around the Holy Spirit; after all, the Spirit leads us into salvation, which is ultimate deliverance from Satan. Satan is diametrically opposed to the Holy Spirit because He is God's representative on Earth.

Consider this: Suppose there was a bridge that could be used to escape your archenemy, and you stumbled upon that escape route. And just imagine that your adversary also knew of this bridge to freedom. Do you think your enemy would leave it alone? No, he is a saboteur, a clever enemy who would stop at nothing to destroy that bridge. The Holy Spirit is your bridge of escape!

From the days of John the Baptist until now, the kingdom of Heaven has suffered violence, and the violent take it by force.

MATTHEW 11:12 ESV

THIRD PERSON

The Holy Spirit is referred to as the third person of the Godhead. He is no less God than the Others, as they are all distinct in function and duty. The Holy Spirit is not *like* God, He *is* God! He is not in third place, or third in importance; each member of the Trinity is co-equal, co-substantial, and co-essential.

Each member of the Godhead has a distinct role: The Father thinks and creates, the Son speaks, and the Spirit moves and carries out what has been spoken. It is a continual fluid love affair within the Godhead, often referred to as "The Divine Dance." In theological terms, the Greek word for this is *perichoresis* or "rotation." It can also be translated "to make room; to give way." Another way of expressing this concept is the phrase "community of being"; each triune person, while maintaining His distinctive identity, penetrates the others and is penetrated by them. As defined by Merriam-Webster's, "to penetrate" means "to see into or through; to discover the inner contents or meaning of; to affect profoundly with feeling; to diffuse through or into." They are fully diffused with one another, profoundly loving and seeing into one another's Beings, without any separation, dark secrets, hidden thoughts or agendas. Isn't this what all of us want? It is found in Him! He invites us into the Divine Romance—fully enveloped, diffused, and imbued with His Spirit! As Paul said to the Athenians, "For in Him we live, move, and have our being..." (Acts 17:28a NIV).

A passage where this perichoretic relationship is seen in sharing their glory can be found in John 17. The Son freely asks the Father to glorify Him with the glory they'd shared before the world began. In John 16, Jesus also says that the Spirit will glorify Him by revealing to us what He receives from Jesus, and that all that belongs to the Father is His. Their glory, Kingdom, and power are equally owned and freely shared with each other.

The Triquetra (or Trinity Knot) pictured above is a symbol used by Celtic Christians since the 19th century. Composed of three separate, intersecting circles, it is figurative of the Father, Son, and Holy Spirit. The parts are separate, yet interlocked in unity, and sometimes shown as below with a circle symbolizing their surrounding love and the unity of the Godhead.

> *Father, the hour has come. Glorify your Son, that your Son may glorify you. I have brought you glory on earth by finishing the work you gave me to do. And now, Father, glorify me in your presence with the glory I had with you before the world began.*
>
> JOHN 17:1,4-5 NIV

Because God is love, this interpersonal relationship of the triune God is never competitive or territorial. In fact, the humility of the Holy Spirit is on display, as His role is always to honor and exalt the Father and Son. His humility should make Him even more attractive to us.

> Whatever God needs to be done, the Spirit is the Doer of it.

The Father, Son, and Holy Ghost each have a divine role to play in the Trinity. They do not compete with each other; they complete each other. The Holy Spirit assists the Father while exalting the Son. He is not less than God, He is equal in essence while subordinate in function. The Spirit works with the Son to accomplish the will of the Father.

The Spirit is the executive agent of the Trinity. Whatever the Godhead needs to be done, the Spirit is the Doer of it. Everything God does in the world must be accomplished by and through the Holy Spirit. The Spirit is what God is doing on Earth! He manifests God's presence while displaying God's power.

The Ontological Trinity

Ontology is concerned with the nature and relations of being. The teaching of the Ontological Trinity refers to the equality of the triune Godhead. It is sometimes called the "'Immanent Trinity." All three persons within the Godhead are equal in nature, essence, and attributes.

Each is God. Each member of the Trinity is equally omnipresent, omniscient, and omnipotent. We understand that each is everywhere, knowing everything, with unlimited power. They each share the same divine nature, and they are equal in glory, power, and wisdom.

> *They are One. They do not compete with each other; they complete each other.*

In contrast to their complete unity and equality, our human nature is driven by competition. We have to know who's the best, strongest, fastest, most important. This can be a problem when studying the Trinity. The Father, Son, and Holy Spirit never strive for supremacy over each other or disagree with each other. They are One. They do not compete with each other; they complete each other. They operate in perfect fluidity.

There is no division, only indivisible Oneness; in mathematical terms, a radical root. The equation looks like this: $1^3 = 1$. Even if you were to cube One, you still have One who is indivisible and whole.

In the Godhead, the measure of importance is only determined by need. Said another way, from the human perspective, the One needed most is most important at that time.

The Economic Trinity

The Economic Trinity focuses on the relationship within the Trinity. It deals with the role of each person within the Godhead and the way they seamlessly cooperate and coordinate within themselves. In simple terms, the concept of the Ontological Trinity looks at the essence of what God *is*, while the Economic Trinity looks at what God *does*. Ontologically, the Father, Son and Holy Spirit are equal but economically, they are distinct.

The term "economic" relative to the Trinity comes from the word *oikonomia*, which is the Greek word for "economy." *Oikonomia* literally means "household management." In the management process, there are roles and protocols. Each person of the Godhead collaborates and contributes in perfect love and fellowship to complete the Trinity.

> Each person of the Godhead collaborates and contributes in perfect love and fellowship to complete the Trinity.

This is confusing to us because in the natural order, the only thing that happens when multiple people are in charge is chaos. The Law of Entropy is defined by *Merriam-Webster's* as "a process of degradation or running down or a trend to disorder." This means that I don't have to plant weeds; I only have to plant a garden and weeds will come naturally. This is evidence of another of Webster's definitions of entropy: "chaos, disorganization, and randomness."

In the world where we live as fallen man, order must be established through effort. Where order is seen, force has been exercised. The supernatural realm is counterintuitive; God's Kingdom is established in love, managed through power, and tends to order. The triune God knows how to perfectly manage His household within their distinctive economic roles.

> God's Kingdom is established in love, managed through power, and tends to order.

The Father creates and thinks, the Son speaks, and the Holy Spirit moves in accordance with the Word. Consider the following scriptures that highlight the differentiation of their personal activities:

The Father sent the Son. (John 6:57)

The Father and Son send the Spirit. (John 15:26)

The Spirit speaks only what He hears. (John 16:13)

> *To God's elect...who have been chosen according to the foreknowledge of God the Father, through the sanctifying work of the Spirit, to be obedient to Jesus Christ and sprinkled with his blood. (1 Peter 1:1-2)*

THE FATHER'S HELPER

In Genesis 24, we are introduced to Abraham's most trusted servant, his household manager. He is endowed with great responsibility, although his name is purposely not stated in this passage. This is because he is anonymously commissioned with a most important task to be done with no glory or honor given to himself. He is trusted, yet still required to swear an oath that he will accomplish the task. The patriarch Abraham will send this reliable servant into a distant land with one objective: He is instructed to find a bride for the son, Isaac. She is to be no ordinary bride, for this is not the beginning of a family, but the beginning of a nation. The faithful servant is entrusted with the future of Israel, God's chosen people.

> *A generous person will prosper, and anyone who gives water will receive a flood in return.*
>
> Proverbs 11:25 ISV

This humble servant is more than a steward, he is an extension of Abraham's name and authority. Amazingly, all of Abraham's resources have been allocated to the servant. He is assigned a blank check.

Fast forward: The perfect candidate is found. She isn't a manipulative gold digger; rather, she volunteers to serve the servant. With no expectation of gain, she carries water for the 10 camels. Experts say a thirsty camel can drink up to 30 gallons (135 liters) in 13 minutes. For 10 camels, that's a total of 300 gallons of water. At 8.34 pounds per gallon, Rebekah may have carried 2,500 pounds of water for a

> Eliezer displays the role of the Spirit as Helper, inviting us into an intimate, covenantal relationship with the Son.

stranger's animals! What a beautiful and selfless servant's heart! Unbeknownst to her, she is watering her own blessing—these camels will belong to her when she and Isaac are wed. She has no idea of the prestigious position she will hold in history. She has been handpicked by the servant, who was directed by God in answer to prayer before he'd even finished speaking it. The perfect match for the son!

The servant lavishes her with many gifts, including golden earrings and bracelets. When she accepts and wears these gifts, her family immediately notices the change. When we receive (spiritual) gifts from God, everyone takes notice. There is no hiding of the Holy Spirit's endowments.

I delight greatly in the LORD; my soul rejoices in my God. For he has clothed me with garments of salvation and arrayed me in a robe of his righteousness, as a bridegroom adorns his head like a priest, and as a bride adorns herself with her jewels.

ISAIAH 61:10 NIV

The servant's name is never mentioned in this entire account, even in conversation with the bride-to-be or her family. He is only referred to as "the servant" or "the man." He never speaks of himself (clue), only referring to the father or the son, continually directing the focus to them but never himself. He craves no notoriety, no credit for his participation. His humility is noteworthy. He is the perfect messenger, an untainted ambassador. He is a type and shadow of the Holy Spirit.

When we study the household of Abraham, we find that he had a chief servant and steward whose name was Eliezer. Interestingly, his name in Hebrew means "God is help" or "Helper of God." As a biblical "type," Eliezer displays the role of the Spirit as God's Helper, inviting us into an intimate, covenantal relationship with the Son. The Holy Spirit is our Helper, sent from God. He helps God toward us, and He helps us towards God. It is believed to be Eliezer's sole responsibility to facilitate the marriage of the son. So it is with the Spirit: He does not speak of himself, He bears precious gifts, and He is the Matchmaker of the Son.

Not only does Eliezer the helper find her, he also lavishes her with priceless gifts (another clue to his identity). That's right — he has many gifts! (The steward took 10 camels from the father's house—1 to ride on himself and 9 to carry gifts. A camel can comfortably carry 330 lbs. for eight hours, and as much as 900 lbs.—there was no shortage of gifts and an enormous dowry to pay for the bride!)

> He knows it's her, obviously, because she is wearing his gifts!

It should also be underscored that when she arrives with the camel train of precious gifts, Isaac is found alone, awaiting his bride, and he runs to her with reckless abandon. Isaac shows no restraint or composure; he impatiently desires to see her, to be with her. Of course there were no cell phones, no selfies, no pictures to describe Rebeccah, but he knows it's her, obviously, because she is wearing his gifts!

As the verse quoted below says of the Spirit, Eliezer takes what he receives from Abraham (the Father) and uses it to find the bride (the church) on behalf of Isaac (the Son of Promise).

> *But when he, the spirit of truth comes, he will guide you into all truth. He will not speak on his own; he will speak only what he hears, and he will tell you what is to come.*
>
> John 16:13 NIV

Pneumatology

We should strive to have the most uncomplicated understanding of the Holy Spirit. Theology may often feel burdensome or challenging, but you may be surprised as you search for truth—it is the Holy Spirit that leads us into it. So even when the content seems a bit academic, your participation in the discovery of truth places a demand on the Spirit. In response to your seeking, He imparts that truth. The goal is to take complicated information and turn it into practical application.

> *He [the Holy Spirit] will glorify me because it is from me that he will receive what he will make known to you. All that belongs to the Father is mine. That is why I said the Spirit will receive from me what he will make known to you."*
>
> John 16:14-15 NIV

Pneumatology is the study of spiritual beings; in biblical context, it is the study of the Holy Spirit. Basically, we are studying the aspects of the Spirit. I am a Trinitarian. This means I believe in God the Father, Jesus the Son, and the Holy Spirit. This belief states that the Godhead is one God in three divine persons. If you try to explain the Trinity you can lose your mind, if you try to deny it, you may lose your soul!

Modern society demands clarity, and avoids the unfamiliar. We are not comfortable with mystery—we want handles and demand answers that line up to our values. When we limit God to what we can understand, we penalize ourselves with gross ignorance.

There is no way to completely and perfectly understand the Trinity. I have been married over 25 years and still have not completely and perfectly understood my wife. The unsolved mysteries don't take away from the marriage, they add to the intrigue and allure of my beautiful bride. The beauty is that I'm still getting to know her. And it is a privilege that I am the one that gets to discover new things about her all the time. After 25 years she is not the same person I married, she is better!

> *Pneumatology comes from the Greek words pneuma (breath, wind, or spirit) and logia (study). As we saw in Chapter 1, the Hebrew word ruach has the same meaning as the Greek. The Spirit is the breath of God, breathing into us!*

"The Spirit reveals, unfolds, takes of the things of Christ and shows them to us, and prepares us to be more than a match for satanic forces."

SMITH WIGGLESWORTH, *"THE TEACHINGS OF SMITH WIGGLESWORTH"*, SIMON AND SCHUSTER, 2013

Actually, I engage in things every day that I don't fully understand. I turn on the computer; I switch on a light. I don't allow my lack of understanding to prevent me from enjoying their benefits. There is absolutely no way to know the Spirit completely, but there is nothing that prevents you from knowing Him truly!

> *"To profess to know a great deal about the Spirit of God is contrary to the nature of the Spirit of God. There is a hiddenness to the Spirit that cannot be uncovered. There is an immediacy of the Spirit that cannot be shoved into vision. There is an invisibility of the Spirit that cannot be forced into visibility. There is a reticence of the Spirit that cannot be converted into openness. For these reasons one feels helpless, inadequate, and unworthy to write a line about the Spirit."*
>
> BERNARD RAMM, SECRET CHURCH, 2008

There is a mystery and majesty of the Spirit that cannot be uncovered by human intellect; it can only be discovered by divine revelation.

THE CORRECTION PROTECTION PLAN

> *Whoever loves discipline, loves knowledge, but whoever hates correction is stupid.*
>
> Proverbs 12:1

The Spirit convicts the world of sin while convincing the world of righteousness. He convicts the world of sin while simultaneously comforting us from the effects of sin. His correction is good. His plan is perfect.

Only a fool considers correction as rejection. Correction is not about rejection, it's about protection.

A car can accelerate to 140 mph. It has brakes because a car can accelerate to 140 mph! The brake pedal is commensurate to the gas pedal. Brakes are not anti-gas, they help to regulate and control speed.

We were born with drives. These compulsions are not all bad, they just need to be in a legitimate context. The Holy Spirit, like pumping your brakes, puts order and control into you're your life. Therefore, your life is not demolished by drives, but determined through disciplines. Correction is not rejection, but protection.

> *He that hath no rule over his own spirit, is like a city that is broken down, and without walls.*
>
> *Proverbs 25:28*

The goldfish felt so restrained in his little bowl. He anxiously awaited the day that he could escape the confines of his prison. He would then go wherever he wanted to, and no one could stop him, no one! Little did he know, his bowl was not correction, it was not even restriction, it was his life-sustaining protection!

The Spirt convicts us of sin; conviction is not condemnation. As people of conviction, we step into our position as God's children. As He convicts us of sin, He is steadily convincing us of His righteousness. This is so that we can live in "right standing" with God.

And when He comes, He will convict the world concerning sin, and righteousness, and judgment.

John 16:8 ESV

Character is exposed by the Holy Spirit, and built through our submission. Character building is an exercise done in the dark.

The Holy Spirit does not isolate us from sin, He insulates us from sin. By His sustaining power, we are in this world but not of this world. His presence is denoted by signs, wonders, and miracles. We ourselves become a sign of the grace and love of God. It is the Spirit that assures us of this and presents us without shame before God.

An Impersonal Force?

If the Holy Spirit was viewed as only a force or energy, wouldn't you feel ridiculous at any attempt at communication? Have you ever had a conversation on the phone, only to realize you're talking to an automated voice system? If you've had this conversation, then you know this feeling. When I do something like this, I immediately look around to see if anyone is watching. We are programmed to be suspicious of any unfamiliar number. I often hesitate, waiting to see if the call is a recording. I hate to feel stupid.

> "We are told to let our light shine, and if it does, we won't need to tell anybody it does. Lighthouses don't fire cannons to call attention to their shining — they just shine."
>
> Dwight L. Moody

Satan uses this to take an advantage against us. Awkward, weird, and goofy are just a few emotions utilized to make us feel gullible and ignorant. He is always working the angles; much research and development has gone into his underlying scheme of creating confusion. Satan is a deceiver, so if he can convolute any aspect of the Spirit's identity, he can reduce your relationship with the Spirit to a game of chance. All he needs to do is create suspicion, which leads to trepidation, which leads to fear, which leads to fallout.

Awareness Inspires Hope

Understanding the third person of the Trinity creates awareness and appreciation of who He is. Awareness is so important because it stimulates interest—God wants your attention. Awareness also conditions us for the next step, acceptance. Awareness prepares us to receive with an open and grateful heart.

When we put God to the side, we are guilty of rejection. Rejection says there is something better for me out there. I know that for some this has never been deliberate. They follow convenience and safety and don't like to be stretched. But, you wouldn't reject a third of anything else in life—why settle for less of God?

> You wouldn't reject a third of anything else in life—why settle for less of God?

The Spirit is the absolute game changer in your life. He is the communication of God. He is also the spell breaker that will transform a dull, anemic existence into a thriving, resilient, and uncommon life. The Holy Spirit breaks the spell of Satan. When we trust the Spirit of truth, the lies of the enemy are exposed. We begin to operate out of confidence rather than fear.

He is no ordinary person. When we desire more of Him, He consumes more of us. Just as fire changes the molecular structure of what it feeds upon, the Spirit changes the one who hosts His presence. Change by natural fire occurs from the *outside in*, an *external force* acting as the catalyst which changes the structure of what is set aflame. Change by Holy Ghost fire occurs from the *inside out*, an *internal force*—just because others can't see it, does not mean it isn't happening. The Spirit is the Change-Agent and Catalyst who sets our lives ablaze, changing us into the very image of Christ!

BECAUSE HE'S IN ME

Is not my help in me? And is wisdom driven quite from me?

JOB 6:13 KJV

We know the Holy Spirit is a person, but do we know He is personal? He is more than just a person; He is the One who has chosen to live *in us*. He calls us His temples wherein His glory dwells.

Do you not know that your bodies are temples of the Holy Spirit, who is in you...?
1 Corinthians 6:19a NIV

...the glorious riches of this mystery, which is Christ in you, the hope of glory.
Colossians 1:27b NIV

When we begin to echo the voice of the Spirit, we invite the process of change. We miraculously develop into the creation we were always meant to be. It becomes evident that the One we host on the inside is navigating our lives to victory. As Paul wrote, "Now to him who is able to do immeasurably more than all we ask or imagine, according to his power that is at work within us, to him be glory in the church and in Christ Jesus throughout all generations, for ever and ever! Amen" (Ephesians 3:20-21 NIV).

Don't allow the voices from the outside to become louder than the voice on the inside. There is a voice, it may be still, it may be small it continually and profoundly dispatches truth, and there is none like it. It is the voice of the Spirit. It is none other than the person of the Holy Ghost. Allow Him daily to speak to and through you.

May the grace of the Lord Jesus Christ, and the love of God, and the fellowship of the Holy Spirit be with you all.
2 Corinthians 13:14 NIV

HIS VOICE IS POWER

Every spell shall be shattered; every lie shall be destroyed. This power is inexhaustible. Like a tsunami, this power cannot be ignored, it must be acknowledged. Satan understands one thing: authority. Your voice has authority; you can exercise this power armed with God's truth over your life. Satan's mouth is open only because your mouth is shut. Quit telling God about your great crisis; tell your crisis about your great God.

But you will receive power when the Holy Spirit comes on you.

Acts 1:8a NIV

Anything of value attracts thieves. Your enemy knows your value, even if you don't. The reason diamonds aren't in convenience stores is because they are valuable. The reason they are valuable is because they are rare. You are rare. You are uncommon.

Speak life over yourself until you're convinced of it. We speak self-fulfilling prophecies. If we make negative declarations, we reap negative consequences. Life follows your voice. You can listen to life, or life will listen to you. The choice is yours.

> *"...Not by might, nor by power, but by my Spirit" says the Lord Almighty.*
>
> *Zechariah 4:6*

You shall also declare a thing, and it will be established for you: So light will shine upon your ways.

Job 22:28 NKJV

I make a conscientious choice to speak blessing over my life. I declare a preferred outcome. My life will be evidence of God's favor. The closest mouth to my ear is my own. I will ascribe and adhere to the Sprit's voice of victory and not defeat! When armed with truth, you are no longer pitiful but powerful. Lies are easily identified. The enemy's cryptic schemes must be disclosed, unable to lurk in dark details. Plans for your ruin are spoiled, and weapons are rendered helpless. Just as light dispels darkness, truth cancels the lie.

The tongue has the power of life and death, and those who love it will eat its fruit.

Proverbs 18:21 NIV

THE ANSWER TO PRAYER

The Holy Spirt is here, not as a last resort but as a first response. He is completely God and completely here. We cannot do the work of God apart from the power and presence of the Holy Spirit. To try to operate without Him is futile, pointless, and powerless.

> The antidote for the disconnect between God and man is the third person of the Trinity.

He prevents distance from God, while accessing all of Heaven for our benefit. When you neglect Him, you avoid nearness to God while inviting distance. When distance is conceived, it gives birth to indifference, and indifference is extremely dangerous! The antidote for the disconnect between God and man is the third person of the Trinity.

In Exodus 33, God offers blessings and protection to Moses apart from presence. Moses is not ok with this. In his respectful protest, he longs for presence; "Not without you," Moses declares. He lets God know, "This is non-negotiable; we must have You!"

In the Old Testament, walking with God was a privilege few got to experience. Because of the third person of the Godhead, we can all now walk in the presence of God. We don't have to contend for His presence! God is on location; He is here — no contest! We are a people He won't forsake with a promise He won't forget.

And I will ask the Father, and he will give you another advocate to help you and be with you forever—the Spirit of truth. The world cannot accept him, because it neither sees him nor knows him. But you know him, for he lives with you and will be in you.

JOHN 14:16-17 NIV

Chapter 3

POWER ON
FIRST RESPONSE

WHAT DEFINES A FIRST RESPONDER?

First Responder: a person who is likely to be among the first people to arrive at and assist at the scene of an emergency such as an accident, natural disaster, or terrorist attack.

> *"Not by might nor by power, but by my Spirit," says the LORD Almighty.*
>
> ZECHARIAH 4:6B NIV

Tim is a powerful minister in our church who weekly ministers to the incarcerated. In Dayton, Ohio, you have a garden variety of inmates. There are those arrested and charged with petty crimes as well as those charged with major crimes, such as murder. Tim has done this for years and can tell "war stories" you wouldn't believe. Like someone standing and urinating in the middle of his message, or men who curse him while he volunteers to be there for them. He is often unappreciated and unrecognized, though he leads repentant men to God by the dozens. No doubt, his reward is coming!

Supernatural Power on Earth

One evening when Tim entered the jail, he saw another member of our church on duty in the facility. Dustin was the corrections officer and in charge of the pod in which Tim would soon be ministering.

> The Holy Spirit is our Champion. He is the First Responder to all of life's difficulties.

Before Tim could set up to minister, an inmate walked out of his cell on the second floor. He pulled out his bed sheet that he'd fashioned into a noose and placed it around his neck. He jumped! He dangled tethered to the hand railing, suspended between floors. As the officer in charge, Dustin must follow protocol and get every man back into his cell. He must secure the three floors while attempting to attend to the man hanging between floors.

Tim responds quickly and, while standing on a sink, he grabs the man's ankles and knees. With adrenaline surging, he hoists the limp body as high as possible. Dustin has swiftly implemented the lockdown policy and reaches down from the second floor. Miraculously, he is able to untie the knot and release the man. Paramedics are quickly on the scene. And believe it or not, he survives!

What an illustration of God's grace and mercy! What an example of first responders! Tim had planned to preach about Lazarus' resurrection from the dead that night, but the Holy Spirit knew what needed to be spoken. He later said to me, "I didn't even get to preach my sermon" to which I replied, "Oh, you preached all right! A powerful sermon with a powerful illustration—life!"

And if the Spirit of him who raised Jesus from the dead is living in you, he who raised Christ from the dead will also give life to your mortal bodies because of his Spirit who lives in you.

ROMANS 8:11 NIV

The Holy Spirit is our Champion. He is the First Responder to all of life's difficulties. He empowers us with life and all things that pertain to it. He helps us to do what we alone could never do. He brings *extra* to our *ordinary* and *super* to our *natural*. We are not confident because of our ability; we are confident because of His authority!

A Real Superhero

I remember watching an old Superman episode. When I say "old," I mean original. It was black and white, and Superman was a tall, husky, barrel-chested man with jet-black hair.

He was foiling a robbery. Gangsters dressed very nicely back then, with three-piece, pinstriped suits and low-brimmed hats. They looked a lot like attorneys, but being gangsters, their nefarious activities drew the attention of our superhero and a fight ensued. In the middle of the scuffle, they wielded their guns and began to fire off rounds. The special effects department, well, let's just say they weren't that good. Every time a gangster fired his pistol, a little spark of light would appear on Superman's chest. Sometimes in the same spot — imagine that!

> *The Spirit's actions are consistent with His abilities. He does not make false claims — He always comes through!*

And the Oscar goes to…

After they had unloaded their guns, one of the bumbling robbers took his gun and had the audacity to throw it right at Superman's head - right at his signature black curls! Nooo! Thankfully, Superman ducked right in the nick of time. Honestly, he ducked! It missed him because he ducked. Did I mention he ducked?

Something's not right with this image. My brain is conflicted. He just repelled bullets to his frontal torso, and he ducks to avoid an 8 oz. piece of metal thrown at 10 mph! Bottom line, his abilities were inconsistent with his actions!

When the enemy shall come in like a flood, the Spirit of the LORD shall lift up a standard against him.

Isaiah 59:19b KJV

Unlike this dated Superman movie character, the Holy Spirit is consistent with His power, protection, and guidance. He does not make false claims. He always comes through!

For no matter how many promises God has made, they are "Yes" in Christ. And so through him the "Amen" is spoken by us to the glory of God.

2 Corinthians 1:20 NIV

Jesus said to him, "If you can believe, all things are possible to him who believes."

Mark 9:23 KJV

The one who calls you is faithful, and he will do it.

1 Thessalonians 5:24 NIV

Belief is Backed by Behavior

Even though we have been prone to neglect the Spirt, He has patiently waited for our communication and participation. Even when we hesitate, that nudge, that prompting is His invitation to come.

"God loves each of us as if there were only one of us."

SAINT AUGUSTINE

To recap, if there is no interest, there is no entrance. Choosing to avoid the Spirit is a decision; searching for God is an inherent instinct. Human beings have an innate hunger for spiritual interaction, whether they know it or not.

MY CONFESSION

As I studied the Trinity, something began to come alive in my spirit. Honestly, because of the ambiguous nature of the Trinity, for years I just filed the whole study away in a box called "faith." In fact, I had no problem believing; the problem was *what* was I believing? Could I explain my belief? But in my case, this box called "faith" was becoming the junk drawer. The place I put things that I didn't know what to do with.

Making peace with apathy results in tragedy. Carelessly, I had ignored the promptings of the Spirit. Like playing hide and seek, He wanted me to find Him. And, by finding Him, I would come to know Him more.

> *Making peace with apathy results in tragedy.*

You will seek me and find me when you seek me with all your heart.

JEREMIAH 29:13 NIV

Keep asking, and it will be given to you. Keep searching, and you will find. Keep knocking, and the door will be opened for you.

MATTHEW 7:7 ISV

So there I was, not confused but a little puzzled. I grew up in church, which was great, but often led to just believing without much debate or understanding. This is referred to as "blind faith." If you ever had questions, you sometimes felt you were not walking by faith. Truth is, questions are good. What can't be tested can't be trusted. Answers don't naturally appear out of thin air. Answers don't follow *you*, answers follow *questions*.

If you call out for insight and cry aloud for understanding, and if you look for it as for silver and search for it as for hidden treasure, then you will understand the fear of the Lord and find the knowledge of God. For the Lord gives wisdom; from his mouth come knowledge and understanding.

PROVERBS 2:3-6 NIV

I began to feel like maybe, just maybe, I should know more. At the least, I should *desire* to know more. I even felt a little guilty, as if I were questioning my formal and informal training. Nevertheless, something kept calling. I find it hard to explain but maybe you've experienced the same conundrum?

So, as I voluntarily went deeper, not just through experience but through education as well, I have come to find a deeper and more profound understanding of the Spirit. Now I don't just rest on what I have been *told*, but on what I *know*. Now I have a desire to know him even more.

I want to know Christ—yes, to know the power of his resurrection and participation in his sufferings, becoming like him in his death.

PHILLIPIANS 3:10 NIV

I know whom I have believed, and am convinced that he is able to guard what I have entrusted to him until that day.

2 TIMOTHY 1:12B NIV

NECESSITY OF THE SPIRIT

"Earthly wisdom is doing what comes naturally. Godly wisdom is doing what the Holy Spirit compels us to do."

CHARLES STANLEY, WALKING WISELY: REAL GUIDANCE FOR LIFE'S JOURNEY, THOMAS NELSON, 2006

Mom Prays, Dead Son Comes Back to Life

"'He was dead for 45 minutes.' That's what the doctor who treated 14-year-old John Smith said after paramedics rescued the teen who spent 15 minutes submerged in an icy lake. Dr. Kent Sutterer and his team performed CPR on John for 27 minutes with no success. The question was raised: how long should they continue?

"His mother then came into the room and started praying loudly. What happened next, defies explanation. 'I don't remember what all I said,' recalls John's mother, Joyce Smith. 'But I remember, "Holy God, please send your Holy Spirit to save my son. I want my son, please save him,"' she said.

"'They hadn't been getting a pulse at that time, so all of a sudden I

Supernatural Power on Earth

> "Holy God, please send your Holy Spirit to save my son...," she said.
>
> Dr. Garrett said, "It's a bona fide miracle."

heard them saying, "We got a pulse, we got a pulse.'" His heart restarted.'"

"Doctors were worried how much brain function he would have, but at this point it doesn't seem like there will be a problem. He's recovering, walking and getting physical therapy. Dr. Garrett said, 'It's a bona fide miracle.'"

(Online source: Kay Quinn, "Mom Prays, Dead Son Comes Back to Life", *USA Today* (2015), accessed September 26, 2017, https://www.usatoday.com/story/news/2015/02/04inspiration-nation-mom-prays-son-back-to-life/22883985/)

Deep calls to deep in the roar of your waterfalls; all your waves and breakers have swept over me.

PSALM 42:7 NIV

THE PARACLETE WALKS ALONGSIDE YOU

Unaccepted by the world, unseen by the world, but known by you. This is the Comforter Jesus promised in John 14:16: "And I will pray the Father, and he shall give you another Comforter, that he may abide with you forever." The Greek word for Comforter is *parakletos*. The Holy Spirit is your "Paraclete." This means "to come along beside, to encourage, to comfort, to be an advocate, an intercessor." The word translated as "Comforter" in this KJV quotation is translated as Paraclete, Advocate, and Counselor in other versions. The Holy Spirit advocates for us and counsels us; He stands by us and for us. The Holy

Spirit clears the way or makes the way clearer. The Holy Spirt is first on the scene, aiding us, protecting us, guiding us.

> The Holy Spirit stands by us and for us. The Holy Spirit clears the way or makes the way clearer.

We use the prefix "para" in many common words. Para- is defined "beside, alongside of, beyond." Examples might be paramedic (a medical professional who works alongside a doctor in a subsidiary or accessory capacity), parachute (a device to support and slow your descent preventing death), and parable (an allegory which runs parallel to or alongside truth). These are also examples of what the Paraclete does: He comes alongside us to support, uphold and slow our descent, give us wise counsel, and reveal truth.

THE SPIRIT IS FIRST ON THE SCENE

The Holy Spirit is first on the scene. The third person in the Trinity is the First Responder. According to the Ontological Trinity, God in three persons is there; but according to the Economic Trinity, the Holy Spirit is the first on assignment. This is His role, His duty. He is the Helper. He is our Protector and Promoter. The Holy Spirit secures our defense and sanctions our success.

> *I will ask the Father, and He will give you another Helper, that He may be with you forever; that is the Spirit of truth, whom the world cannot receive, because it does not see Him or know Him, but you know Him because He abides with you and will be in you. I will not leave you as orphans; I will come to you.*
>
> JOHN 14:16-18 NIV

THE PARACLETE INTERCEDES THROUGH US

> *By His Spirit he hath garnished the heavens; his hand hath formed the crooked serpent. Lo, these are parts of his ways: but how little a portion is heard of him? but the thunder of his power who can understand?*
>
> JOB 26:13-14 KJV

How little a portion is heard of Him? Fascinating! He is not a secret tunnel that leads to great treasure, He is the *only* way to that treasure. He is the one that provides access to and entry into the things of God.

It's early Friday morning and Robin, who attends our church, is preparing for the day. With a house full of kids, there's never enough time and always more to do. She hears the care flight emergency helicopter flying overhead. This is common; they fly that route often. What is uncommon is her response. She goes out to the porch, and with a fervent burden she raises her hands toward the emergency helicopter. Passionately she begins to intercede. She prays with intensity for God to spare life. The Spirit within her has arrested her attention. All day she prays; she will not understand why this moment is so vital until Wednesday evening.

> The Spirit within her has arrested her attention.

On the same early Friday morning, Jarred, a care flight nurse that also attends our church, is headed to the scene of a life-threatening automobile accident. The helicopter ambulance has arrived—it is used only in critical situations, so these situations often end badly. A young man is being pulled from the wreckage. Jarred does not recognize the young man he is treating with the most urgent care. As a first responder, Jarred has seen a lot of tragedy—it's par for the course. But this time, something unusual is going on; Jarred will not understand the full ramification of his service until Sunday.

On his way to school early that Friday morning, Rieley, a high school senior that attends our church, is about to have a near-death experience. As he drives, he loses control when his car hits the freshly laid gravel. His car slams into a telephone pole. Paramedics will have to use the Jaws of Life to cut him out of his car. He is in critical shape: He has broken teeth, a broken nose, and multiple breaks in his arm. Along with many cuts and bruises, there is something underlying that has not yet been discovered: His collision with the telephone pole was so hard that his aorta, the main artery to his heart, has been torn. In a matter of minutes, he could have bled out and died. But God had a different plan! Like a bowl, the empty cavity of his body formed into a reservoir. Here the blood collected and applied pressure to the leaking aorta, preventing fatal hemorrhaging. A miracle!

Five days later on a Wednesday, I stood with Rieley in church to testify of God's goodness. In Sunday's service, we again stood together to give God glory. On Wednesday, Robin sees why she was compelled to intercede. On Sunday, Jarred is amazed to see God providentially work through his own life, and the testimony goes full circle throughout our church.

The Spirit of God is the First Responder, working supernaturally throughout the ways of man. He is guiding and guarding on a consistent basis. Whether we see it at first glance or not, we cannot deny the effects of His supernatural power on Earth.

The wind blows wherever it pleases. You hear its sound, but you cannot tell where it comes from or where it is going. So it is with everyone born of the Spirit.

JOHN 3:8 NIV

HEAVEN TO EARTH TO HEAVEN

Every day we benefit from the mysterious workings of God. I want to look at the function of the Trinity from another perspective. From our perspective, Heaven looks down upon the earth. So we view the Godhead from a Heaven to Earth perspective.

From Heaven to Earth, we would view the Trinity in this order: Father God first, Jesus the Son second, and the Holy Spirit third. In fact, this is why He is called the third person of the Trinity. For emphasis, I repeat: Third person is not third place. The Father, Son, and Spirit are co-equal, co-substantial, and co-essential — They are One.

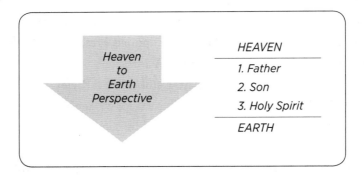

Now I want to challenge your thinking. We know that critics ask questions, but thinking people also ask questions. Asking questions is a sign of a disciple. The only dumb question is the one you don't ask. How does the Trinity look from an Earth to Heaven perspective? I'll introduce the same example from a different view. I want to look at the same example but from a different perspective. This time we will view the triune Godhead from Earth instead of from Heaven.

Power On First Response

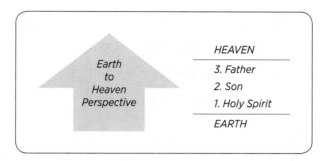

From Heaven to Earth, God the Father is always in first place. But from Earth to Heaven, something interesting takes place—a new dynamic, maybe even a new revelation. Viewed from Earth to Heaven, the Holy Spirit is first. This is not a challenge for preeminence, it's just a fact when position and perspective are taken into consideration.

For man to get to God we must go through the Spirit first. Even if you were unaware of this model at salvation, this process took place. No one comes to God except the Spirit draws him. It is impossible to receive eternal salvation apart from the Spirit. The Spirit is the entry point into the presence of God.

Until the Spirit is poured on us from on high, and the desert becomes a fertile field, and the fertile field seems like a forest.

ISAIAH 32:15 NIV

Isaiah uses desolation and ruin as a metaphor. "Until" tells us we don't have to continue living barren, unproductive lives. The Spirit comes bringing favor and blessing. We become productive like fertile, fruitful fields. The *Jamieson-Fausset-Brown Bible Commentary* says it this way: "The barren shall become fruitful by regeneration; those already regenerate shall bring forth fruits in such abundance that their former life shall seem but a wilderness where no fruits were."

THE SPIRIT BREATHES LIFE INTO MAN

Then the LORD God formed a man from the dust of the ground and breathed into his nostrils the breath of life, and the man became a living being.
GENESIS 2:7 NIV

God formed man and man was beautiful, but he was in form only. From Earth, God molded and formed this exquisite representation of Himself to bring Him glory. But he was just a form, like an empty glove. Lifeless, unanimated, until…

The first of the Godhead to meet Adam was none other than the Holy Spirit. Of course, God the Father formed Adam, but Adam received awareness by the Spirit. God breathed (Hebrew *ruach*), and man became a living soul. Adam is met first by the Holy Spirit. From Earth to Heaven, the Spirit is always first. Until you are brought to life by the Spirit's work in your life, you are comatose and lifeless. But when awareness comes, a bold, new world is opened unto you.

The Spirit of God has made me; the breath of the Almighty gives me life.
JOB 33:4 NIV

Like the first responder paramedic who does "mouth to mouth" to bring consciousness, the Paraclete breathes life, consciousness of God, and ongoing life support to those who welcome His entrance. He is so much more than the third person of the Trinity — He is the First Responder of Heaven!

Chapter 4

POWER ON
THE HIDDEN SPIRIT

Truly you are a God who has been hiding himself, the God and Savior of Israel.

ISAIAH 45:15 NIV

If the Holy Spirit is always there, why do I sometimes feel alone? As a pastor, I have heard this question many times. The silence of God has always been an enigma. Every believer feels that God is distant at some time or another. Seasons of silence can be frustrating unless you understand the nature of God. There are many reasons we experience what we perceive as distance from God. We may be dealing with guilt or habitual sin. Or, in His providence, God may be preparing us for something greater He has in mind for us. God is always up to something. His greatest work is often accomplished behind the scenes.

SIN SEPARATES

But your iniquities have separated you from your God; your sins have hidden his face from you, so that he will not hear.

ISAIAH 59:2 NIV

Where sin is prominent Satan is dominant. So, what is sin? Sin is broken relationship with God. Sin is disobedience to Gods' word, His way, and His will. Sin gives opportunity and advantage for demonic control in your life. And by the way, we have all sinned.

If I had cherished sin in my heart, the Lord would not have listened...

PSALM 66:18 NIV

> Jesus called the Holy Spirit "the Spirit of truth." He will not play along with our charade.

Jesus called the Holy Spirit "the Spirit of truth." This is important to know. He will not play along with our charade. It may be easy to fool others, but our pseudo personality is unacceptable to the Spirit. He can distinguish between the testimony and the "testiphony." Everything is open and naked before God's eyes. There is full exposure in the presence of God.

I'm sure you've heard someone lie, and you know they're lying, and *they* know *you* know they're lying. You know that feeling of insult coupled with frustration. It's not a good feeling. For me, it leaves an awkward angry feeling.

He is the Spirit of truth. When truth is compromised, the Holy Spirit withdraws Himself. We may feel He has ignored or abandoned us. Not true. He is leading us away from thoughts, motives, or behaviors that grieve Him so that our fellowship with Him will be honest. All things come clean before the Spirit. When we engage in sin the Holy Spirit then backs away. David referred to this in Psalm 51:11.

Do not cast me away from Your presence, and do not take Your Holy Spirit from me.

PSALM 51:11 NKJV

Fortunately for us, the path back is short and direct; it's called repentance. This is what the apostle Paul called "godly sorrow"—it results in a change of thinking and behavior. In contrast, "worldly sorrow" may be weeping tears, experiencing guilt, shame, or remorse, but the inner man continues to think the same way about the sin and outwardly, the behavior is unchanged. Indicators of true repentance are not how long or loud you cry or how badly you beat yourself up, it's that you simply change your way of thinking, then turn and walk in the direction the Spirit is going so that He can go alongside you. (Remember, He's the Paraclete, called alongside us—that means we should be in unwavering march step with the Spirit.)

Yet now I am happy, not because you were made sorry, but because your sorrow led you to repentance. For you became sorrowful as God intended and so were not harmed in any way by us. Godly sorrow brings repentance that leads to salvation and leaves no regret, but worldly sorrow brings death.

2 CORINTHIANS 7:9-10 NIV

God never turns away from brokenness. Where sin abounds, grace is in much more abundance. Repentance is always met with forgiveness. God's forgiveness is a powerful and unrelenting force. His love is wild and boundless and cannot be contained. Forgiveness will knock

> Even when you have felt isolated and deserted by God's Spirit, you are not.

down anything that stands in the way of repentance. Rest assured, when you sincerely repent, you are completely forgiven. No exceptions!

Even when you have *felt* isolated and deserted from God's Spirit, *you are not.* For instance, you may feel abandoned right now, but you are not. As you opened this book, you opened your heart. You weren't *pushed* to read these pages, you were *pulled* to read these pages. Think about it—even now God's Spirit is engaging with your spirit.

The Spirit entreats us to pursue His presence even when we're void of feeling. Most faith walks are not accompanied by feeling. Operating under emotion compromises faith. According to God's word, without faith we cannot please God. Don't rely on emotions or feelings – ground your faith in His faithful promises to never forsake you and to be with you until the end!

INTO THE DARKNESS

God called the light "day," and the darkness he called "night." And there was evening, and there was morning—the first day.

GENESIS 1:5 NIV

From the earliest account of creation, we understand that every day begins with nightfall. For devout Jews, Friday at sunset is the beginning of Sabbath, which is observed on Saturday. When we count our days we start with morning. When God counts days He starts with the night. With God, we always end in light.

The path of the righteous is like the morning sun, shining ever brighter till the full light of day.

PROVERBS 4:18 NIV

Farmers will tell you that a seed must be planted under soil where it's pitch-black, void of light from the seed's perspective. There it will remain alone, in the dark, below the surface. Understand this: We are not *isolated from* potential, we are *insulated to* potential. There is great potential within the seed, merely waiting for the right time for germination and growth. Seasons of what may feel like isolation are seasons of germination.

> Seasons of what may feel like isolation are seasons of germination.

Nature constantly reminds us of Gods ambiguous, yet rewarding, ways. Crops grow taller under the canopy of darkness. Plants receive sunlight for energy. Through photosynthesis, plants will store energy from the sunlight during the day. At night, they will convert that energy into sugars and water, which will be used for food. In the case of grass, most growth occurs right before dawn. How do we expect growth, if we never experience darkness?

For his anger lasts only a moment, but his favor lasts a lifetime; weeping may stay for the night, but rejoicing comes in the morning.

PSALM 30:5 NIV

In a spiritual sense, we often endure long nights. There may even be seasons where we feel we've lost our way. We can't abandon in the night what God has given in the light.

But if I go to the east, he is not there; if I go to the west, I do not find him. When he is at work in the north, I do not see him; when he turns to the south, I catch no glimpse of him. But he knows the way that I take; when he has tested me, I will come forth as gold.

JOB 23:8-10 NIV

NOT HIDDEN FROM YOU, HIDDEN FOR YOU

An Australian couple*, Terry and Anna, had been dating for over a year. Terry had come to the conclusion, "she's the one." As he contemplated the process of engagement, he decided to use his own artisanship and creativity. He bought a traditional engagement ring, then crafted a wooden pendant to conceal the costly ring. He attached the pendant to a necklace and presented this as a gift to Anna. He asked her to wear it always; even though it wasn't very expensive, it was created from his own hands.

Every day for more than a year, she wore the costume jewelry with the costly ring concealed inside. For a year Terry would record Anna as she wore the necklace in order to archive the time and events surrounding his concealed treasure and her faithful commitment. Every day, she thought he was just recording her, which was true, but he was also monitoring his investment in her. Unbeknownst to her, he was keeping an eye on her hidden treasure.

A treasure is anything a person greatly values. It is uncommon and treated as precious. Something may have great monetary worth, but not be treasured. Something which has no material value may elicit strong emotional attachment and be a priceless treasure to the beholder.

At the end of the year, not tracked by her but from the time she received the pendant, Terry took Anna on an exotic vacation to Scotland. While sightseeing, they visit a 'smoo' cave. This is a large sea cave that combines both salt and fresh water. In natural terms, two separate streams of water are blended into one.

For a whole year, Anna has consistently worn a hand-carved necklace that would be considered cheap to the untrained eye. That is, the eye that could only see from the outside. Terry asks for the necklace, and with a knife he unlocks the treasure hidden in the pendant. The cheap trinket carved from huon pine was the container for the exquisite diamond that had been in her possession the whole time.

> *The cheap trinket carved from huon pine was the container for the exquisite diamond that had been in her possession the whole time.*

The whole event had been predestined. The trip, the cave, the proposal. Oh, and if you're wondering, the word 'smoo' is an old Norse word that means 'hidden'. How clever is that?

*Source: *Independent,* Rachel Hosie, Published May 11, 2017 (http://www.independent.co.uk, accessed online 10/14/17)

THE PLEDGE OF HIS PROMISE

The story of Terry and Anna has another interesting twist—it can be seen as a "type" or picture of the relationship between Christ and the church. He has hidden a treasure in you! God has concealed a treasure of inestimable value in the hearts of believers—His Holy Spirit as an "engagement ring." The apostle Paul explained this to the believers at

Supernatural Power on Earth

> God has concealed a treasure of inestimable value in the hearts of believers — His Holy Spirit as an "engagement ring."

Corinth when he wrote, "He who prepared us for this very purpose is God, who gave to us the Spirit as a pledge." (2 Cor. 5:5). The Holy Spirit within is our engagement ring, sealing and setting us apart, the symbol of His pledge that He will redeem us and take us unto Himself.

The word Paul chose to use in this verse and the two following is *arrabon*. In his book, *Ephesians* (New York, T&T Clark International, 1998, pg. 151), Ernest Best attests that *arrabon* "is a legal and commercial term of Semitic origin adopted into Greek which commits both giver and recipient to the completion of a deal under penalty. Yet the earnest is not just a pledge or guarantee that something will be given later; it is itself a partial gift..." This term was common in Jesus' day and is still used in today's Grecian culture. The word has an intimate quality in addition to usage for commercial agreements.

The arrabon of modern Greece has to do with the engagement period prior to an actual wedding. It is the betrothal period, and is itself a formal ceremony. It takes place among the relatives of the contracting parties and is looked upon almost as binding as the actual wedding itself. Unlike a commercial down payment, the agreement has a covenantal aspect; like the cutting of a covenant in ancient times, breaking of the agreement results in severe penalty.

"If we went to Greece today and met an engaged lady and asked to see her arrabon, she would put out her hand with an engagement ring on it. In modern Greek, that is what the word means." (William Allen Johnson and Holt N. Parker, *Ancient Literacies: The Culture of Reading in Greece and Rome*, (New York, Oxford University Press, 2009, pg. 26.)

In reference to the Spirit, consider the following quote: "He [the Arrabon] is the heavenly Lover's engagement ring given to us. We shall carry that engagement ring with us into God's future, when we have the full wedding ring of final union with Christ." (Michael Green, *I Believe in the Holy Spirit*, Grand Rapids, Michigan: William B Eerdmans Publishing Company, 2004, pp. 101, 102.)

He anointed us, set his seal of ownership on us, and put his Spirit in our hearts as a deposit, guaranteeing what is to come.

2 Corinthians 1:22 NIV

That [Spirit] is the guarantee of our inheritance [the firstfruits, the pledge and foretaste, the down payment on our heritage], in anticipation of its full redemption and our acquiring [complete] possession of it—to the praise of His glory.

Ephesians 1:14 AMPC

Paul further explained, "But we have this treasure in jars of clay to show that this all-surpassing power is from God and not from us" (1 Cor. 4:7). Like Anna, who wore the ring concealed within a simple wooden pendant, we carry the promise of the Father, His very own glory, within unassuming "jars of clay," earthen vessels hiding a treasure undiscerning eyes can't see.

The secret of the LORD is for those who fear Him, and He will make them know His covenant.

Psalm 25:14 NASB

Like Terry recording Anna, God carefully watches over those who carry the Holy Spirit. The Spirit is the earnest, or down payment, of betrothal until our Bridegroom comes to take us to the Father's house for our wedding ceremony. The gift of the Holy Spirit, the Arrabon, is a foretaste of Heaven and eternal union with our Beloved, fully realized at the consummation of our marriage with Christ.

Then I heard what sounded like a great multitude, like the roar of rushing waters and like loud peals of thunder, shouting:

"Hallelujah! For our Lord God Almighty reigns. Let us rejoice and be glad and give him glory! For the wedding of the Lamb has come, and his bride has made herself ready. Fine linen, bright and clean, was given her to wear."

(Fine linen stands for the righteous acts of God's holy people.) Then the angel said to me, "Write this: Blessed are those who are invited to the wedding supper of the Lamb!" And he added, "These are the true words of God."

REVELATION 19:6-9 NIV

GOD'S SILENCE IS NOT GOD'S ABSENCE

We are victims of discouragement when we operate only from the outward appearance. We must operate on principle rather than appearance. In principle, we understand that God is always working things out for our good.

> God works out everything in conformity with the purpose of His will.

Did you know that according to Ephesians 1:11, God works out everything in conformity with the purpose of His will? The intricate designs of God's plan are not always made plain. We often hope the Holy Spirit would just directly intervene, but He seems to remain silent and aloof.

According to Romans 8:28, situations and events are working together to complete a preferred outcome. Circumstances overlap and underlap, weaving together a purpose far greater than we can recognize at first glance.

For we are God's handiwork, created in Christ Jesus to do good works, which God prepared in advance for us to do.

EPHESIANS 2:10 NIV

What God desires from us is faith—faith to believe the impossible. Faith honors God and God honors faith. Faith pleases God. Our faith produces the victory that overcomes the world.

God wastes nothing. No pain, no trial, no difficulty. The Spirit of God is working throughout every situation for a better outcome, which may yet be unperceived. Many times, I've learned this lesson only after complaining, then regretted my childish behavior thinking, "If only I would have had more faith and been more patient." When we become aware of the interplay of God's Spirit, we become confident in God's timing and convicted by His purpose.

His radiance is like the sunlight; He has rays flashing from His hand, and there is the hiding of His power.

HABAKKUK 3:4 NASB

A Dreamer's Nightmare

One of the most obvious examples of deferred blessing is found in the life of Joseph. His life-struggle and triumph is a type and shadow of Christ. Like Jesus, he was the beloved son of his father. Joseph was the suffering servant despised and rejected by his brothers. Later, as prime minister of Egypt, we see his kindness and forgiveness displayed as he provides life essentials to those who meant him harm.

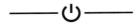

Delayed hope makes the heart sick, but fulfilled desire is a tree of life.

PROVERBS 13:12 HCSB

Joseph's father blessed him with a special coat of distinction. This coat of manifold colors is commensurate with the manifold grace the apostle Peter speaks of: "As each one has received a gift, minister it to one another, as good stewards of the manifold grace of God" (1 Pet. 4:10). As we grow into our coat, we also grow in God's grace.

Joseph's coat was made by his father. It was not dyed fabric but swatches of different colors and textures. Like our lives, many colors comprise the garment the Father has created for us: bright and cheerful colors, muted colors of boredom, dark colors of conflict. Many trials deserve the credit for the uncommon design of your life. You may not be satisfied with your history, but it is your unique history that helps shape your destiny.

> *You may not be satisfied with your history, but it is your unique history that helps shape your destiny.*

The colorful coat of distinction created many problems for Joseph. The preferential treatment he received from his father came at a price.

His brothers were indignant towards him. He shared dreams of pre-eminence that further fueled their envy and hatred. This accelerated and accentuated a deep contempt that invoked hostility.

Joseph had a dream, and when he told it to his brothers, they hated him all the more.

GENESIS 37:5 NIV

POTENTIAL IS DISGUISED BY WEAKNESS

The profound conflict in your life isn't about where you are, but where you can be. Almost anyone can recognize a towering oak with vast branches, but few can see that same tree in a little acorn. Satan attacks us early. He comes in waves long before we come into our relevance and giftings. He maligns and assaults us while we are premature and manageable. For Satan knows that when *we* know what *he* knows, *he's defeated.*

But you have an anointing from the Holy One, and all of you know the truth.

1 JOHN 2:20 NIV

A true nightmare is the frustration of a dream that never manifests. We can become overly time-conscious and miss the big picture. The critical factor that separates many of us from our dreams is simply time. Time becomes foe rather than friend. King David declared to God, "my times are in Your

> Given the same treatment, if you were thrown into that pit would it now be empty?

hands." And his son, King Solomon, said "all things are beautiful in their time."

To a fault, Joseph seemed to be oblivious to his sibling's frustration until they turned on him. The original plan was just to kill him but, after a single protest, they settled to throw him into an empty pit and sell him to foreigners as a slave. Given the same treatment, if you were thrown into that pit would it now be empty? Or would it be full of rage, resentment and revenge? When I think of Joseph's struggle, it becomes incredibly hard to have my own "pity party."

I am certain he didn't feel so special at this juncture, as his lucid dreams had implied.

In Joseph's case, we are given the unique perspective of hindsight. We see his undesirable journey of scandal and betrayal become the divine transportation to his unprecedented destiny. On the backside of history, we understand the Spirit's developing process. If only we had the foreknowledge to look ahead and praise our way through the process!

GOD IS WITH ME

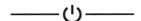

A man once said, "I knew there was a God, but did He know there was a me?"

Joseph's life is divided into scenes — from the pit to the palace, his struggle is unrelenting although Joseph never appears to complain or give up. It's as if he had read the final chapter in advance.

He is an overachiever, even under unbearable resentment, accusation, and misrepresentation. In every sordid scene, Scripture gives this comforting disclaimer: "But God was with him." This speaks of the Holy Spirit's work in your life. Through the person of the Holy Spirit, God is always with you.

And I will ask the Father, and he will give you another advocate to help you and be with you forever— the Spirit of truth. The world cannot accept him, because it neither sees him nor knows him. But you know him, for he lives with you and will be in you.

JOHN 14:16-17 NIV

Joseph is experiencing a sovereign detour. No amount of prayer or fasting will deliver you from a sovereign detour — this is God's doing. And, whether you like it or not, it will accomplish a divine purpose. No one's standing in line in hopes of the next sovereign detour. But, when it is completed, you wouldn't trade the experience for the world.

I consider that our present sufferings are not worth comparing with the glory that will be revealed in us.

ROMANS 8:18 NIV

Joseph found himself as a servant to Potiphar. He quickly moved up the ranks to become chief among the household servants. He was always promoted; no matter where he was he would find favor. The scripture says repeatedly, "God was with him." Did he know this? Could he feel this? Rejected, abused, and displaced—how could this possibly be a "God thing?"

Potiphar's wife continually attempts to seduce Joseph. When he rejects her advances, she accuses him of rape. So off to prison he goes. But God was with him.

On and on his story goes, years expire with no justice. How could he ever be exonerated? DNA hasn't even been discovered yet; this has got to be the most unfortunate individual alive. But God was with Him!

Literally, the future of the world is at stake. Then it happens, out of nowhere, or absolutely out of somewhere, the tables turn.

> Look up, let faith rise — you may have the correct address, just unaware of the promotion that's coming!

Pharaoh is troubled by dreams he knows to have significance, but his questions are unanswered. There is only one man alive that has the answer — he just happens to be sharing the same royal address but with a different view and accommodations. He's *under* the palace, in the royal prison. Look up, let faith rise — you may have the correct address, just unaware of the promotion that's coming!

One of Joseph's former cellmates tells Pharaoh that he knows a man that can interpret his dream. Joseph had done this for him when he was in prison. In his trusted position of chief cupbearer, this prisoner just happened to have Pharaoh's ear.

Pharoah calls for Joseph, who gives him the dreams' meanings. His divinely inspired interpretation will save the Egyptian kingdom, as well as Joseph's own family and the people of Israel, from death by the coming famine.

WHAT CAN'T BE TESTED CAN'T BE TRUSTED

And He called for a famine upon the land; He broke the whole staff of bread. He sent a man before them, Joseph, who was sold as a slave. They afflicted his feet with fetters, he himself was laid in irons; until the time that his word came to pass, the word of the LORD tested him.

Psalms 105:16-19 NIV

Now the code is being cracked, the enigma has been solved. Joseph was sent ahead! Sent where he would have never ventured. Whatever you label it, the broken road, the road less travelled, it all makes sense now. He is sent into a foreign country via contempt, conflict, and controversy. He would never wish this upon himself but God, Who is sovereign, has willed this upon him.

Get this straight: Joseph is not in the palace as a reward for his faithfulness. He is there for his kindred's unfaithfulness. He is not there to save his life; he is there to save the world. The world is dying of starvation, and God has one man set aside with the skill set necessary for the world's redemption. When I begin to think of what the Spirit's objective is towards you, I can only think of one word— hallelujah! God is more than the defender of the just, He is also the defender of the unjust! His plan is for good. He is sovereign and just.

> *His plan is for good. He is sovereign and just.*

THIS TIME IT'S FOR GOOD

There is a day of reckoning where Joseph's brothers stand before him. Shamefully they bow before him, just as his adolescent dream foretold. Regret, maybe? Humiliated, definitely! They are humbled before this most powerful man they unconscionably abused. Motivated by fear for their own lives, they repent of their evil. But see Joseph's gracious words to his treacherous brothers:

> *But as for you, you meant evil against me; but God meant it for good, in order to bring it about as it is this day, to save many people alive.*

GENESIS 50:20 NKJV

The Hebrew verb "meant" traces it's meaning back to the word "weave." This means that what his brothers had woven for evil, God had woven for good. God is in full control of the warp and weft of our lives.

When we view the backside of a tapestry, we only see tangled threads with no apparent pattern. But on the other side, a beautiful design has been created.

[He has sent me to] provide for those who grieve in Zion—to bestow on them a crown of beauty instead of ashes, the oil of joy instead of mourning, and a garment of praise instead of a spirit of despair.

ISAIAH 61:3A NIV

The robe of recognition Joseph's father had created for him was woven with purpose. Every color of his life would be intricately woven together to create a preferred outcome. Encrypted into that coat was a distinguished calling. His life was not one-dimensional but multi-faceted. Other lives were dependent upon his existence, including ours.

> He is not hidden from you, He is hidden for you!

Eventually his torn and tattered robe, becomes an exquisite royal robe. We must be convinced that God is supernaturally weaving His glorious, mysterious plan for our good. That time, this time, and every time, it's for good!

Even through times of difficulty and distance, the Spirit of God is working around the clock on your behalf. The Spirit is scanning the earth to bring to pass the divine purpose for your destiny. He is not hidden *from* you, He is hidden *for* you!

For the eyes of the Lord run to and fro throughout the whole earth, to show Himself strong on behalf of those whose heart is loyal to Him.

2 Chronicles 16:9a NKJV

Chapter 5

POWER ON
THE ANOINTING

⎯⎯ ⏻ ⎯⎯

But my horn shalt thou exalt like the horn of an unicorn: I shall be anointed with fresh oil.

Psalm 92:10 KJV

The Oil of Gladness

The origin of anointing was from a practice shepherds used to delouse sheep. Insects were a constant threat to sheep as they fed. Mosquitos and biting flies would constantly attack the flock. Lice and other insects would burrow into the sheep's wool, causing irritation and disease. The sheep's ears, nose, and eyes were especially vulnerable to dangerous infestation. When attacked by such pestilence, a lamb could actually beat it's head to death. This is an example of what a satanic attack can inflict upon a person who is not under the protection of the anointing. Shepherds poured oil onto the head of the sheep as a repellent. The slick application would protect the sheep from the troublesome annoyance. From this early practice, the anointing became symbolic of protection.

Sovereign LORD, my strong deliverer, you shield my head in the day of battle.

Psalm 140:7 NIV

This treatment was referred to as "the oil of gladness," which Israel's King David would have applied to the sheep when he was a young shepherd. In their prophetic song, David's psalmists wrote of this oil in Psalm 45, which the writer of Hebrews 1:9 linked to Christ's anointing as the eternal King of kings.

Your throne, O God, will last for ever and ever; a scepter of justice will be the scepter of your kingdom. You love righteousness and hate wickedness; therefore God, Your God, has anointed You with the oil of gladness more than Your companions.

Psalm 45:6-7 NKJV

Anointed for Service

In the passage above, "therefore" implies that your anointing and gladness is directly relational and proportional to your love of righteousness and hatred of wickedness. The Holy Spirit helps us to desire holiness and have a distaste for unrighteousness; this will keep our hearts full of the gladness and joy of the Lord, which is our strength and power for the service He's called us to.

In the Old Testament, an anointing oil was used to consecrate and ordain the prophet, priest, or king. This consecration set them apart unto their office of authority. During this religious ceremony, a compound of spices in olive oil would be rubbed or smeared onto the candidate as a type of inauguration. This would be an outward sign of an inward transformation, an endorsement of the highest validation. To be anointed was to be conformed for and dedicated to the service of God. Through this humbling rite of passage, legitimacy was established. However, it was possible to be anointed by God before the formal process of being ceremonially recognized by others.

The anointing oil itself should not be viewed as a magic formula. The anointing oil is merely a symbolic representation of God's stamp of approval and distinction for service. Still today, God's anointing is His endowment and endorsement for service. The anointing separates one for uncommon purpose. Just as the high priest in the Old Testament was set apart, the anointing of the Holy Spirit defines your purpose and directs your destiny. This special anointing inspires us to pursue God with intensity. The Spirit then reveals and releases special ability to perform what once was impossible.

> *God's anointing is His endowment and endorsement for service. The anointing separates one for uncommon purpose.*

THE HOLY ANOINTING OIL

Make these into a sacred anointing oil, a fragrant blend, the work of a perfumer. It will be the sacred anointing oil.

EXODUS 30:25 NIV

God gave Moses a distinct "pattern" for the tabernacle and all of its furnishings. This blueprint was designed with you in mind, for today *we* are the tabernacle. In this process He also gave Moses a detailed recipe for the anointing oil compound. This is symbolic of the precious ointment every believer is qualified to receive through His Spirit.

Supernatural Power on Earth

> *But you have an anointing from the Holy One, and all of you know the truth…As for you, the anointing you received from him remains in you, and…his anointing teaches you about all things and as that anointing is real, not counterfeit—just as it has taught you, remain in him.*
>
> 1 JOHN 2:20, 27 NIV

> The precious ointment is symbolic of the anointing each believer is qualified to receive through His Spirit.

God carefully instructed every aspect of this compound. As you will see, each ingredient and measurement holds detailed meaning.

There are four principal spices that make up this ointment: 500 shekels of pure myrrh, 250 shekels of sweet cinnamon, 250 shekels of sweet calamus, and 500 shekels of cassia. (A shekel is a Hebrew measure weighing nearly ½ ounce.) These principal spices were compounded and then combined with a hin (Hebrew measure of 6.06 liters) of olive oil. Each element was carefully chosen for its unique quality and fragrance.

While studying the measurements, we conclude that there is a total of 1500 shekels. Divide this by 250, your will see that the compound is made of six measures. Two parts plus one, then one part plus two, or 500 plus 250 then 250 plus 500. So, there are 6 parts or measurements of the spices. Six, of course, is the number of man. All four of these blended spices are required in order to produce the genuine anointing.

Then comes the oil. Symbolic of the Spirit, it takes the oil to complete the anointing. The seventh part must be present. Seven is the number of God, the number of perfection. As we carefully examine each part of the ointment, you will see God's perfecting hand at work in your life through your unique, personal experiences.

Pure Myrrh

The myrrh tree grows in the Arabian desert to approximately 8 feet tall. A symbol of suffering and brokenness, its crooked branches gives it a shrub-like appearance.

Its sap is gummy and becomes hard as it is exposed to air. This sap was commonly referred to as the "tears of the tree," as incisions were made in the bark to allow the sap to weep out. This may also explain the literal meaning of the Hebrew word *mowr*, which means "bitterness."

Myrrh was widely used in incense, perfume, and for embalming. It was an antiseptic and disinfectant. It was used as a painkiller as well — by refusing the mixture offered at the cross, Jesus chose to bear not only the sin but also the pain of its penalty.

> *Myrrh was used as a painkiller; by refusing the mixture offered at the cross, Jesus chose to bear both the sin and the pain of its penalty.*

Myrrh was costly and a fitting gift for a king—the wise men brought it to Jesus along with gold and frankincense. Perhaps this gift foretold the bitterness, tears, pain, and death He would bear for us all.

For this first principle spice, I must place emphasis on the adjective "pure." Pure, as in not diluted or mingled. Purity is a topic not embraced by many believers today. Understand this: I love the grace of God, but grace is not the license to sin. God still demands that His chosen people be holy.

You are to be holy to me because I, the LORD, am holy, and I have set you apart from the nations to be my own.

LEVITICUS 20:26 NIV

Purity attracts the anointing of God. Purity invites favor to abide over one's life. Purity is the antidote for regret, while impurity attracts regret. Impurity crowds out the presence of God and deafens your ears to His voice. The greater the purity in your life, the greater the presence of God in your life. Purity begins in private but ends in public. Virtue is rehearsed privately then rewarded publicly.

It is God's will that you should be sanctified: that you should avoid sexual immorality; that each of you should learn to control your own body in a way that is holy and honorable…

1 THESSALONIANS 4:3-4 NIV

> The anointing gives us the power to resist temptation and restore order to our private lives.

As long as you live on this earth, there will be a continual war between your flesh (your human nature) and your spirit. Oscar Wilde said, "I can resist everything, except temptation." The truth is, you will deal with competing loyalties your whole life. Purity may be recognized publicly, but it is only produced privately. The last bastion of privacy is in your personal thoughts. Uncontrolled thoughts lead to an uncontrolled life. When you're born, you look like your destiny, but when you die, you look like your decisions.

The Anointing

The Bible speaks of King Saul's reign that was eventually replaced by God's chosen king, David. King Saul is a type and shadow of operating under the flesh (carnality). And Scripture tells us that there was long war between the house of Saul (representative of your flesh, or fallen, carnal nature) and the house of David (your renewed, born-again spirit). This is indicative of our constant battle to overcome the flesh. Victory over your flesh does not come without a fight. Your flesh, like King Saul, is a "mad man" capable of ten thousand evils. Fortunately, the house of Saul is getting weaker while the house of David is getting stronger. The anointing gives us the power to resist temptation and restore order to our private lives.

You, dear children, are from God and have overcome them, because the one who is in you is greater than the one who is in the world.

1 JOHN 4:4 NIV

The anointing of the Holy Spirit (of Whom the oil was a picture) declares freedom and preeminence over your life. The Spirit crowds out every advance of the enemy while giving control over your mind, will, and emotions. "There is not a square inch in the whole domain of human existence over which Christ (the Anointed One), Who is sovereign over all, does not cry, Mine!" (Abraham Kuyper, "Sphere Sovereignty," in *Abraham Kuyper: A Centennial Reader*, Grand Rapids, MI: Eerdmans, 1998, 488.)

Myrrh was also used in the burial preparation as an embalming agent. So myrrh is symbolic of death. The first step in living as a Christian is to die; we are to die to our

> Myrrh is symbolic of death — we are to die to our flesh daily.

flesh daily. It is difficult to have a proper theology when controlled by a "meology." Self must die according to God's word. As a believer in Christ, our daily challenge is not to live but to die!

The Amplified Bible gives clarity to the apostle Paul's words on this aspect of the Spirit's anointing. As we willingly lay down our own will to the Spirit's will, the sweet fragrance is noticed by both God and others.

For we are the sweet fragrance of Christ [which ascends] to God, [discernible both] among those who are being saved and among those who are perishing; to the latter one an aroma from death to death [a fatal, offensive odor], but to the other an aroma from life to life [a vital fragrance, living and fresh]. And who is adequate and sufficiently qualified for these things? ... always carrying around in the body the dying of Jesus, so that the [resurrection] life of Jesus also may be shown in our body. For we who live are constantly [experiencing the threat of] being handed over to death for Jesus' sake, so that the [resurrection] life of Jesus also may be evidenced in our mortal body [which is subject to death].

2 Corinthians 2:15-16, 4:10-11 AMP

SWEET CINNAMON

Sweet cinnamon is symbolic of God's grace. The cinnamon tree is an evergreen, which means it's always in season. Grace must always be in season to the believer. The cinnamon tree begins very small but through the years, it grows to reach upwards of 30-foot high. In fact, it never stops growing. When it stops growing, it stops living. This is why the apostle Peter exhorts us to grow in grace.

The Anointing

> *But grow in the grace and knowledge of our Lord and Savior Jesus Christ. To him be glory both now and forever! Amen.*
>
> 2 Peter 3:18 NIV

Cinnamon is ground from the bark of the tree. To produce the unique sweetness of God's anointing, we too must experience the grind. Tough times don't last, tough people do.

My wife and daughters enjoy getting their nails manicured together. Apparently, from overhearing their conversations, this can be a painfully good experience. The nails are filed and roughed up in order to create a surface that the polish will adhere to. Like the work of the Spirit, this grinding process is necessary to remove the old layers in preparation for the new growth.

Cinnamon is sweet. Alone, cinnamon is overbearing. Actually, it's no good alone. However, when it accompanies something else, it's amazing! The anointing God has designed for your life, well, how can I say this? It's not just for you! It becomes sweet as it complements others. When the Spirit's gifts begin to operate in your life, they will not lie dormant. Gifts are for the Body and to attract unbelievers. The anointing, when shared, becomes the conduit for God's sweet presence to be enjoyed by all.

> *When shared, the anointing becomes the conduit for God's sweet presence to be enjoyed by all.*

> *Now to each one the manifestation of the Spirit is given for the common good.*
>
> 1 Corinthians 12:7 NIV

SWEET CALAMUS

Calamus is a reed also known as the sweet flag. If you've ever felt stuck in the mud, consider the calamus. It doesn't just survive in the mud, it thrives in the mud. By the way, there's power in the mud!

Can the rush grow up without mire? Can the flag grow without water?

JOB 8:11 KJV

> God's grace teaches us to be more loving and less judging, creating a healthy growth environment, which is firm yet flexible.

It's counterintuitive that mud is vital, even *necessary* for calamus to grow. Mud allows for flexibility while remaining grounded. If it weren't for the mud, the wind alone would break the calamus before it would have the opportunity to become mature. Many who experienced inflexible, rigid beginnings often revolt, fleeing direction because it looks like discipline. Their early stages were legalistic, too restricting, and over-demanding. Legalism leaves behind a wake of hurting and confused victims. God's grace teaches us to be more loving and less judging, creating a healthy growth environment that is firm yet flexible.

When the storms come, and they will, the calamus is brought low. This low position of humility actually protects the reed from straight-line winds. Humility is not demeaning. As commonly attributed to C.S. Lewis, "Humility is not thinking less of yourself but thinking of yourself less." (This is actually a quote written by Rick Warren in *The Purpose-Driven Life,* Day 19, "Cultivating Community." This quote is

The Anointing

an adaptation of what Lewis wrote in *Mere Christianity*, "The Great Sin": "A truly humble man...will not be thinking about humility: he will not be thinking about himself at all.") Humility is not denying that God is on your side, it is acknowledging that God is on your side. Humility produces protection. Pride repels God, but humility attracts God.

Though the Lord is on high, yet He regards the lowly; but the proud He knows from afar.

PSALM 138:6 NKJV

Humility relies on the Holy Spirit. You can trust the Holy Spirit without having humility, but you can't have humility without trusting the Holy Spirit. Humility is a necessary ingredient for the anointing.

Humility has the appearance of being brought low, but this is counterintuitive, for when we are weak God is strong. The storm winds may bring you down for a time, but after a few moments under the sun, you'll rise again.

Calamus, like bamboo, has many uses. One in particular is irrigation. The ancient irrigation system was manufactured as one reed was fitted to another. Biblically, this is referred to as "touching and agreeing." Through unity and the power of agreement, we become the pipeline of blessing; we are literally the Spirit's conduit of power, love, and healing. This underscores the importance of praying together in intercession. If one can chase a thousand, two can chase ten thousand. That is a tenfold blessing!

> *We are literally the Spirit's conduit of power, love, and healing.*

Every section of the reed has a barrier that must be broken to allow the flow of water. Your adversary, the devil, continually erects little

Supernatural Power on Earth

walls to prevent the Holy Spirit's flow into your life. When we get "breakthrough," obstructions are removed and the refreshing anointing can nurture and sustain us with life-giving waters.

Water will gush forth in the wilderness and streams in the desert. The burning sand will become a pool, the thirsty ground bubbling springs. In the haunts where jackals once lay, grass and reeds and papyrus will grow.

Isaiah 35:6b-7 NIV

Calamus, like cinnamon, is very sweet. The sweetness of cinnamon is in the taste, and the sweetness of calamus is in the aroma.

But thanks be to God, who always leads us in triumph in Christ, and manifests through us the sweet aroma of the knowledge of Him in every place.

2 Corinthians 2:14 NASB

CASSIA

The cassia plant is an herb that roots in damp areas close to rivers. Psalms chapter one says that the blessed man shall be like a tree planted by rivers of water.

That person is like a tree planted by streams of water, which yields its fruit in season and whose leaf does not wither - whatever they do prospers.

Psalm 1:3 NIV

"Cassia" is translated from Hebrew to mean "to shrivel up, to bow the head, to stoop." This word has been translated into Greek as to "cleave." Of course, we understand "cleave" as having two opposite meanings: to cut or separate, or to adhere or hold close. Jesus demonstrated this opposite lifestyle on Earth. He was a King that came as a servant. He would be brought low through crucifixion, only to be exalted to the highest place. He would put others first while simultaneously being above all. As we cut away (cleave) from our old man (sin nature), we also cleave (adhere) to Christ's forgiveness and tender mercies. Through His eternal redemption, we can cling to Him and not let go!

Cassia has purple flowers that speak of royalty, but are low in height to represent humility. It is from these flower buds that the fragrant oils are extracted.

Cassia was useful in scenting garments. Psalm 45:8 states that Jesus' robes smell of cassia. This is also a necessary ingredient of the oil of gladness, which sanctified and set our Savior apart.

> *Cassia has purple flowers that speak of royalty, but are low in height to represent humility—from these flower buds the fragrant oils are extracted.*

How God anointed Jesus of Nazareth with the Holy Spirit and power, and how he went around doing good and healing all who were under the power of the devil, because God was with him.

ACTS 10:38 NIV

The roots of the cassia plant are especially noteworthy. They provide support and nourishment despite unsure terrain. These tenacious fibers refuse to lose their grip despite the riverbank's shifting and unstable footing. They establish themselves deeply and firmly. We, like the apostle Paul, "take hold of that which took hold of us." The anointing helps us to strike our roots downward while bearing much fruit upward.

Once more a remnant of the kingdom of Judah will take root below and bear fruit above.

ISAIAH 37:31

A benefit of tenacious roots and fruitfulness is that our "fruit," or children, will also experience the blessing of God. He's promised that they will thrive in His waters. Like the willows and reeds that grow near waters, they hold the banks of the stream to prevent loss of the land. By remaining firmly rooted, they exert opposition to destructive and eroding forces, preserving Kingdom culture for future generations.

For I will pour water on the thirsty land, and streams on the dry ground; I will pour out my Spirit on your offspring, and my blessing on your descendants. They will spring up like grass in a meadow, like poplar trees by flowing streams.

ISAIAH 44:3-4 NIV

Many lose heart too early. The Bible is replete with examples of those who have become faint. They fail to recognize that the dark, downward process is essential for the upward, revealing confirmation. No one can rise up, without first establishing a foundation. The deeper the foundation, the larger the construction.

Your fruits will validate you, but your roots will sustain you. It has been said that your fruitfulness is directly relational to your "rootfulness." Remember, when you see anyone successful at any given thing, there is always more below the surface than what's above.

"Patience, persistence and perspiration make an unbeatable combination for success."

NAPOLEON HILL, MINDSET STACKING™
INSPIRATIONAL JOURNAL *VOLUMESS02*, P.6

The apostle Paul said to his apprentice Timothy, "I know you…you share the same sincere faith that was in your grandmother Lois, and in your mother Eunice." Paul clearly inferred, "I know you because I see you through your roots." The roots that are hidden influence the fruit that is seen. Good roots produce good fruit.

BOTCHING THE BATCH

In ancient Israel, God used Samson to be His judge (a deliverer of Israel), empowered with tremendous physical strength to defend Israel. Though Samson was a powerful champion, his unreliable character brought him down. He was his own worst enemy. He could not manage his beguiling desires. He repeatedly compromised the vows he had made to God, and his lack of restraint led to loss of his anointing for power.

In the New Testament, the Greek word *akrasia* is translated as "self-indulgence" and "excess." It's also defined as "the inability to maintain control; without self-control and hence mastered by personal appetites (urges)" and "lack of power." The result of living self-indulgently is to live without strength and to lack the Spirit's power.

> *The result of living self-indulgently is to live without strength and the Spirit's power.*

Samson is the perfect example of this principle. The Spirit of God would move upon him, and he would perform incredible feats of strength like killing lions, lifting city gates, and defeating armies. But when seduced, he was wavering, unreliable, and eventually weakened.

Satan will not sign a non-aggression agreement with you. If you don't embarrass the temptation, the temptation will embarrass you. Any thought you refuse to take captive will refuse to allow you peace. You have a personal responsibility to yourself. You are the gatekeeper of your own mind. Samson's destiny was hijacked by his unrestrained desire. In a moment of weakness, he reveals the secret — his Nazarite vow. He had not yet broken the part of the vow to refrain from cutting his hair. His long hair was the outward symbol of the consecration upon his head. You, like Samson, are responsible for protecting your head

> Samson's life lesson teaches us that dishonoring one's sacred commitments and living self-indulgently is the recipe for failure — a botched batch of anointing oil.

Samson's hair was not his strength; his hair represented his vow to God. His vow was his strength, the spring of his supernatural power. We often define sin as a certain trespass, but sin actually takes place in the mind before the act of commission. Sin is broken relationship with God, not merely the outward, visible act. Samson's life lesson teaches us that dishonoring one's sacred commitments and living self-indulgently is the recipe for failure—a botched batch of anointing oil. It must be without mixture, pure, and wholly devoted to the Lord.

The undertaker gets to bury his mistakes; unfortunately, we have to live with ours. As Samson's hair was cut he was immediately rendered inoperative. The mighty Samson is bound and eyes gouged out. He is a feeble laughingstock. Shamefully, he is the daily entertainment for his enemies as he pushes at a gristmill, bound like a beast of burden. This is what disobedience looks like. Blind and bound, the wheel goes round and round in a debilitating, cyclical pattern of failure. Samson is forced to walk over his same footprints again and again. This is a life of shame, filled with regrets. The scenery never changes. Repeatedly, he struggles to carry a difficult burden, never able to reach a finish line. What a waste.

Not every trial is due to personal sin. I am aware that some have been victimized. Some have been subjugated to hardship, abuse, or mistreatment. But God sees and knows — He is a Defender and a Redeemer. Satan desires to take strong men and make them weak, while God desires to take weak men and make them strong.

You may be thinking, "If I don't make progress, it's because my past left me powerless." Don't use your history to excuse your failure. True victims need to know that daily decisions can actually change the future. God loves to champion the underdog. Today, the victim line is long and crowded. When you understand the truth of God's redemptive power, your life experience may explain your behavior but it doesn't excuse your behavior.

Do not gloat over me, my enemy! Though I have fallen, I will rise. Though I sit in darkness, the Lord will be my light.

Micah 7:8 NIV

What the enemy did not understand about God's covenant was this: Though we break our vows, God keeps his covenant! God doesn't *act* faithful, He *is* faithful. Our God is a Covenant-keeping God. And His covenant is fulfilled through — you guessed it — His Spirit! When we confess and forsake our sin, we are immediately brought back into right relationship with God. Confession is necessary; unconfessed sin is unforgiven sin. Return. That's it—the blood of Jesus does the rest.

Return to the stronghold, you prisoners of hope. Even today I declare that I will restore double to you.

ZECHARIAH 9:12 NKJV

Through Samson's disobedience, failure was imminent. Through Christ's obedience, grace was abundant. Samson's strength was interrupted but not terminated. God's mercies fail not. We've all struggled with our flesh. I've found myself keeping score of how good I've been. I've even told the Lord, "I'm doing good," only to find myself failing again. I've come to understand that it's not about doing good, it's about doing right.

For the Lord God is a sun and shield; the Lord will give grace and glory; no good thing will He withhold from those who walk uprightly.

PSALM 84:11 NKJV

Samson's power had been obstructed by his own actions, but because of God's mercy, his power would return. Samson sat in darkness, but now the Lord would be his light. Satan had underestimated the vow; though Samson failed to keep his side of the pledge, God kept His. And He always will! Samson's hair had been cut, but his roots were still intact. He still had ROOTS! Never underestimate the power of strong roots.

The Anointing

> *Now this I know: The LORD gives victory to his anointed. He answers him from his heavenly sanctuary with the victorious power of his right hand.*
>
> PSALM 20:6 NIV

THE OIL

The myrrh, sweet cinnamon, sweet calamus, and cassia were compounded and then mixed with a specific measure of olive oil. The oil is symbolic of the Holy Spirit. The oil blends us all together. We are beautifully diverse but the oil makes us one — now we can flow together. Satan uses our differences to divide us. God amalgamates where Satan segregates.

MAN CAN'T CHOOSE WHO GOD'S GOING TO USE

The Prophet Samuel is instructed by God to go to the house of Jesse. From his sons God will choose the next king of Israel. Samuel asks that Jesse's sons be bought to him. Samuel believes he sees the next king. "It must be Eliab," Samuel thinks to himself. As Jesse's oldest son, he looks the part. But God stops Samuel before he makes a colossal mistake.

> *But the LORD said to Samuel, "Do not consider his appearance or his height, for I have rejected him. The LORD does not look at the things people look at. People look at the outward appearance, but the LORD looks at the heart."*
>
> 1 SAMUEL 16:7 NIV

Supernatural Power on Earth

As the strong, young prospects are vetted, God answers the prophet with a resounding "No!" Probably embarrassed to press the issue, Samuel asks Jesse, "Are all of your sons here?" And just like that, we understand how easily we can get lost in the shuffle. Nevertheless, the Spirit searches and marks chosen vessels for the anointing oil. God has a "ways and means" committee, the Holy Spirit, and He has fresh oil ready to pour into any willing vessel.

David the shepherd boy is summoned from obscurity to renown. When Jesse raised the horn of oil over Jesse's other sons the oil refused to cooperate, but now the oil is ready to flow.

So Samuel took the horn of oil and anointed him in the presence of his brothers, and from that day on the Spirit of the LORD came powerfully upon David.

1 Samuel 16:13 NIV

THE OLIVE PRESS

> The olives were crushed, then pressed by heavy weights that were placed upon it. In the same way, Jesus was crushed under the burden of our sin. He not only died for us, He died by us.

The oil specified for use in the anointing compound was derived from the olive fruit. The fruit is shaken violently from its tree, disrupted and separated from the familiar. The fruit would be crushed and then pressed by heavy weights that were placed upon it. In the same way, Jesus was separated from His heavenly dwelling to be crushed under the burden of our sin. He not only died *for* us, He died *by* us. The early Moravians would say we are "the reward of His suffering." He did this for us. Through substitution, He vicariously took our sin while simultaneously imparting to us His righteousness. This is what Martin Luther called "The Great Exchange." The righteous demands of a just God were satisfied at Calvary's cross.

Jesus spends his last hours before the cross in the Garden of Gethsemane. The word "Gethsemane" comes from two Hebrew words, *gath* and *shemen*, literally translated "press" and "oil." Gethsemane means "oil press" and this is where the fruit of the olive was crushed to extract its precious oil. Here, Jesus will be pressed beyond measure. He will pray the Father's will above His own. He will face such extreme spiritual warfare that He will sweat great drops of blood. Here the oil must and will be released. Jesus, Who is the divine perfumer, endures the cross and despises the shame. Jesus models the power of the anointing as He pays the price for our salvation. The anointing flows through Him as He pays our penalty and purchases our freedom.

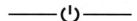

But He was pierced for our transgressions, He was crushed for our iniquities…Yet it was the Lord's will to crush him and cause him to suffer, and though the Lord makes his life an offering for sin, He will see his offspring and prolong his days, and the will of the Lord will prosper in his hand.

Isaiah 53:5a, 10 NIV

When the anointing oil was poured over an individual in the Old Testament, the oil ran over the head and down the body, representing the consuming power of God. The ceremony was very similar to a modern baptism, one with oil rather than water. We know historically

Supernatural Power on Earth

> God's Spirit is not just symbolically poured over you, He enters into you.

that this act was powerful and impressionable, but it quickly dissipated.

Today, God's Spirit is not just symbolically poured *over* you, He enters *into* you. The anointing is not optional, it's essential. The anointing is the Holy Spirit's supernatural enduement, endorsement, and enablement. He permeates you, inside and out. If with exuberance you voluntarily respond to His calling, you too can be empowered by this precious anointing. God will sanction your success, and just like the prophet, priest, and king, you will operate under a new, fresh anointing.

You were slain, and with your blood you purchased for God persons from every tribe and language and people and nation. You have made them to be a kingdom and priests to serve our God, and they will reign on the earth.

REVELATION 5:9B-10 NIV

Chapter 6

POWER ON
IDENTITY

WHO AM I?

Who am I? This is the age-old question of identity. Many have endeavored to discover who they are, only to find themselves even more confused. Through the practice of self-examination minds becomes frozen because the criteria we are given is more than we can process. God has created us as a complex mosaic. We study our actions, our abilities, and our loyalties. Like the cultic "navel gazers" entranced with themselves, we get nowhere. We are advised to "look deep," which supposedly leads to self-improvement, yet ultimately leads to humanism. In fact, we can't look *inward* for identity, we must look *upward*.

The Holy Spirit is God's agent for identity. The Spirit is our aid in our continual search for identity and purpose. It is the Spirit Who helps us to discover our true identity, based in our legitimacy as God's children. We are God's offspring. Identity is not based upon what we can or can't do; it is based upon Whose we are. Surprisingly, our identity is not based upon the talent we possess but in the confidence we have as God's very elect. Identity is validated by position, not possession.

> *Identity is validated by position, not possession.*

Some have settled for believing that their identity is connected to their own decisions. We've all made some bad decisions. It's been said that "we are the sum total of the decisions we have made," that decisions determine destiny. Though we rise out of the carnage of our choices, do they define who we are? Have our bad decisions imprisoned us to a life sentence of hopelessness? I refuse to believe that.

THE PRODIGAL HEART

In Luke 15, the Bible relates a parable about a prodigal son. The word *prodigal* means "waster." We can all relate to this "waster." There are some things in life that we will never get back. However, Scripture tells us that after epic failures and disappointment the prodigal "comes to himself." Himself? So who was he during all of his bad decisions? Clearly, he wasn't himself. He was the consequence of poor decisions. He was an imposter! But, that was never his true identity. My identity holds the secret to my purpose. I am not defined by my past; I am defined by my purpose.

> I may be a product of my past, but I am not a prisoner of it.

Now if Satan has his way, your life will always be in limbo. Even after you've accepted Christ, you will find yourself continually circling back, fighting demons you have already conquered, lingering far too long on the battlefield called regret. There is a fine balance between memory and destiny. This is just one more ploy at defeating your purpose by defaming your identity. I may be a product of my past, but I am not a prisoner of it.

Forget the former things; do not dwell on the past.

ISAIAH 43:18 NIV

So who was this prodigal if he was not himself? The definition was not up to his brother; it was not even up to himself. Only the father knew the true identity of his son.

But the father said to his servants, 'Quick! Bring the best robe and put it on him. Put a ring on his finger and sandals on his feet. For this son of mine was dead and is alive again; he was lost and is found.' So they began to celebrate.

Luke 15:22, 24 NIV

He was dead but not anymore. It is the Spirit that compels us to "come to ourselves." The Spirit brings conviction, we bring confession, then God brings resurrection.

If you declare with your mouth, "Jesus is Lord," and believe in your heart that God raised him from the dead, you will be saved. For it is with your heart that you believe and are justified, and it is with your mouth that you profess your faith and are saved.

Romans 10:9-10 NIV

The apostle Peter foretold that in the last days people will be lovers of "self" more than lovers of God. If your focus is on "self," you will never discover true identity. If your focus is on God, identity will come effortlessly. The Holy Spirit will not force you to make the right decisions, but He will enforce the decisions you make.

A Little Water Goes a Long Way

Water is probably the simplest, most primitive way to discover depressed areas. If you want to find the lowest place in a room, just spill some water. The water will respond by rushing to the lowest spot in the room.

Symbolically, water represents the Spirit. God pours out His Spirit to find us at our lowest place. God's Spirit finds our hurt, disappointment, and pain. He fills those areas with His love, comfort, and forgiveness. In the same way, the water of the Spirit rushes to those who are humble, choosing the lowest place rather than exalting and justifying themselves. God's love fills all depressed areas.

All of you, clothe yourselves with humility toward one another, because, "God opposes the proud but shows favor to the humble."

1 PETER 5:5B NIV

Our human nature tells us that nothing is free. We sometimes shy away from blessing in fear of indebtedness. To avoid the quid pro quos of life, we often do without. God does not love you because you're helpless, He loves you because you're precious.

After being baptized, Jesus came up immediately from the water; and behold, the heavens were opened, and he saw the Spirit of God descending as a dove and lighting on Him, and behold, a voice out of the heavens said, "This is My beloved Son, in whom I am well-pleased."

MATTHEW 3:16,17

At the baptism of Jesus, we see the Spirit descending like a dove. The Spirit is not a dove, but compared here as a dove. God's Spirit is God's agent of identification. It is the Spirit that marks us for favor.

At the Jordan River baptism of Jesus, God audibly identifies Him as His own Son. Those around are shocked by the sound; some even think it's thunder. God expresses His affinity toward Jesus, affirming His sonship and lordship.

One of the titles for the Holy Spirit is the Spirit of sonship. The Spirit of God searches for and targets God's children. He bestows legitimacy upon us as we yield to His compelling call. Our illegitimate spirit finds approval and confirmation through God's Holy Spirit. Through this powerful affirmation we are restored; nothing is missing and nothing is broken. The Spirit of sonship reveals our true identity as God's very elect.

For you did not receive a spirit of slavery that returns you to fear, but you received the Spirit of sonship, by whom we cry, "Abba! Father!" The Spirit Himself testifies with our spirit that we are the children of God.

ROMANS 8:15-16 BSB

BROKEN SILENCE

The time between the Old Testament and the New Testament is often referred to as "the 400 years of silence." Obviously, this description is given because God did not speak to the Jewish people for over 400 years. As the Jews awaited the Messiah, God held His peace until one single day of obedience, when Jesus voluntarily offered himself to John to be baptized. At that very moment, the heavens were opened, the Spirit descended, and the silence was shattered. God's thundering voice was heard again.

Now to be technical, God had already cried out thirty years prior to this. Baby Jesus, who is God incarnate, opened his mouth and our redemption story began. The hypostatic union came to be when God became man. The Word became flesh. The Son of God became a Son

> *The Son of God became a Son of Man so that sons of men can become sons of God.*

of Man so that sons of men can become sons of God.

God's Spirit is the agent of identification. When we humble ourselves and avail ourselves to God's control, the Spirit descends. When we respond to the Spirit, the muted heavens will be clearly heard. As the Spirit falls upon us God speaks over us. As we then yield to God, our identity is awakened. We are invited, received, and grafted into the family of God.

POSITION THEN PROTECTION

> *But now, thus says the LORD, your Creator, O Jacob, and He who formed you, O Israel, "Do not fear, for I have redeemed you; I have called you by name; you are Mine! When you pass through the waters, I will be with you; and through the rivers, they will not overflow you. When you walk through the fire, you will not be scorched, nor will the flame burn you.*
>
> ISAIAH 43:1-2 NIV

God makes a very important declaration over us: He says, "You are Mine." Is He embarrassed or ashamed of me? Is He disappointed in me? Am I really His? No, no, and yes.

God's protection is established through position. We may be imperfect as humans, but from a positional perspective, we are the evidence of His ability to perfect the imperfect. In fact, most of the floods, fires, and flames were of our own making. God will save us from anything, including ourselves.

Accepting our destiny from God is also expecting His protection to accomplish it. To the level we are willing to receive, He is able to achieve.

For it is God who is producing in you both the desire and the ability to do what pleases him.

Philippians 2:13 ISV

Identity Theft

An estimated 15.4 million consumers were hit with some kind of identity theft in 2016. This is up from 13.1 million the year before. It is becoming increasingly more common to lose your identity. Despite the many safeguards in place to protect your identity, the persistent thief never stops imagining new and improved ways to take what you have by replacing who you are.

September 11, 2001, will go down in infamy. America became acquainted to terror. As a nation we were blind-sided, although the threat had always been there. This particular event would change the collective mindset of our nation. Our security, our transportation, and our basic way of life would never be the same. This evil left a wake of uncertainty and confusion. There are currently over 1100 unidentified bodies remaining in a New York city morgue — one of the most gruesome events of our day. There are still unanswered questions and charred remains with no identity. How could this be? With modern technology this seems unfathomable. But for those undeserving victims and their bereaved loved ones, we are left speechless. We may never find a match for these unfortunate remains, but God knows. He knows every soul on this planet. He knows where you are and where you should be. Without God, we are helpless, hopeless, and unidentified.

B.K. DOE

Writing in *The New Republic* magazine, November 21, 2016, Matt Wolfe writes the story of B.K. Doe. (Accessed 4/30/18. https://newrepublic.com/article/138068/last-unknown-man.) In 2004, behind a Burger King in Richmond Hill, Georgia, a man was found beaten, naked, and unresponsive. His body was covered by ant bites, as he had been exposed for a long time. Only questions surrounded him, as no one came forward to give any explanations.

When he finally regained his consciousness, he was of no help to the authorities. He knew nothing. Absolutely lost.

He gave himself the name "Benjaman Kyle." because in the hospital he was given the nickname "B.K. Doe." B.K. stands for Burger King. He was utterly confused with no fixed point of reference.

Benjaman was diagnosed with severe dissociative amnesia. He was plastered all over social media, *National Geographic* picked up his story, and he was eventually featured on the *Dr. Phil Show*. No one came forward. It was so sad because not only was he traumatically abused, there was no one that missed him.

> *It is bad never to be chosen; it is worse never to be seen at all.*

The first human dilemma was loneliness, the knowledge of being alone. God saw Adam alone and for the first time declared something of His creation was *not* good. It is bad never to be chosen; it is worse never to be seen at all.

Even in a world of autonomy and self-reliance, it is still terrifying to be alone. Benjaman had FBI fingerprinting and DNA testing, yet he remained unknown for over ten years. When he was reissued a social security number, he jokingly had it tattooed on his backside for precautionary measures. Ironically, most tattoo shops require identification!

LOST IN DISOBEDIENCE

Of course, we know that sin and disobedience leave us empty, searching for identity. We have all experienced a setback, an accident, or just blatant rebellion. We live lives of confusion and contradiction. But when we encounter God's Spirit, direction and clarity lead us so that we are no longer uninformed. We have better information — we have an internal witness.

Obedience is the necessary ingredient for course correction. We not only confess our failures; we forsake our sins. Life is lived at the speed of obedience. Obedience is not only how we get by but how we get ahead.

> *Life is lived at the speed of obedience.*

But maybe this wasn't your fault at all. Maybe you are a true victim. Violated, exposed, left for dead. This is after all, an unconscionable generation. We are capable of a thousand evils. So many have been hurt so badly that identity seems to be the least of their worries — survival is the priority in their life. This may be so, but God does not move by accidents; He moves by providence. You are meant to do more than survive, you are meant to thrive.

After many disappointments expectation becomes dull. This is a natural defense mechanism. Without expectation, we can't be disappointed. We need a resurrection of expectation.

[He] who is able to do immeasurably more than all we ask or imagine, according to his power that is at work within us...

EPHESIANS 3:20 NIV

The Spirit is searching, reaching into dark recesses of our hearts. Liberating those bound and confused, He whispers, "Freedom is here."

Anything of value attracts thieves. You are of great worth; why would you not be Satan's next target? Satan has always desired to meddle with your identity. Most live uninformed of the value of their true worth and unprepared to protect it. It has always been Satan's plan to bring you down; it has always been God's plan to lift you up.

This was the same way Satan operated in the life of Jesus, our example in all things. Remember the words of identification the Father spoke at Jesus' baptism: "This is My beloved Son in Whom I am well-pleased." The record of this event (Luke 3:21-22) is followed by Christ's genealogy, in which His identity is further affirmed by tracing His bloodline all the way back to "Adam, the son of God" (v.38).

> Satan knows that when we know Whose we are and who we are (identity), we will never fail.

Immediately after Chrit's identity was established by His Father, the first verse of the next chapter tells us that the Spirit led Jesus into the Wilderness where He was tempted by Satan (Luke 4:1-13). Twice, Satan whispers, *"If* you are the Son of God..." Notice what's missing? He is the *Beloved Son* of God and His *Father is well-pleased* with Him. The tempter would never mention that! He knows that when we know Whose we are, the Father's great love toward us, and who we are (identity), we will never fail.

Our enemy lies and tells us we're not loved, that God is angry or displeased with us, that we're not good enough or strong enough. Though the Spirit may lead us into the wilderness, He also whispers the Truth to refute the lies so that we won't fail in our temptations either. We will stand strong, knowing our identity as dearly beloved children of God.

As Jesus said, "It is written..."

See what great love the Father has lavished on us, that we should be called children of God! And that is what we are!

1 JOHN 3:1 NIV

And I pray that you, being rooted and established in love, may... grasp how wide and long and high and deep is the love of Christ, and to know this love that surpasses knowledge—that you may be filled to the measure of all the fullness of God.

EPHESIANS 3:17-19 NIV

Like "B.K.Doe," you may have no answer to your dilemma, but that does not exempt you. It may explain you, but it does not excuse you. You have an obligation to humanity, and you owe it to yourself. There has never been anyone like you.

You were created with a signature purpose. The Bible says that all of creation has been waiting for you to be revealed.

For the anxious longing of the creation waits eagerly for the revealing of the sons of God.

ROMANS 8:19 NASB

"When?" Creation cries. "When?" asks Destiny. Your purpose awaits.

PAID IN FULL

Patty Hearst was ransomed for 6 million dollars in 1974. Charles Lockwood was captured and ransomed by an Argentine group twice. The ransom is estimated to be over 50 million dollars in today's currency. Regardless of how many zeros follow these payouts, the greatest ransom ever was paid in full, without any argument. God allowed His Son to be captured, tortured, and slain so that we could be ransomed from torment and death. He did this so that you could be part of His great family. And the Trinity agrees—you are worth it all!

The Holy Spirit is the conviction and confirmation that God is with you and for you. He is present, and He believes you're precious. You're not pure, but you're preserved. You're not always powerful — sometimes you're pitiful, but you're protected.

> You are God's offspring. Even when you've lost your identity, He still knows it.

You are God's offspring. Even when you've lost your identity, He still knows it. And reminds you of it! Too much has been invested in you to go bad. Under self-examination, it's easy to underestimate our value. But when we understand how much we actually cost, we understand our true value. An object is only worth what someone is willing to pay for it.

AS A CHILD

At nine years old, I received the Baptism of the Holy Spirit, with the evidence of speaking in tongues. My experience was the game changer for my life. I know that even as an adolescent, rambunctious boy, the Holy Spirit immediately changed the trajectory of my life. Did I understand it? I understood what a fourth grader understands. I just know that nothing was coerced or manipulated; I needed something and God supplied it. Whatever had happened was so real that to this day I have a complete recall of the entire event. There are so many things at nine years old that I don't remember, but this is not one of them.

The evangelist gave an altar call, and I piled myself up to the right side of that oak pulpit. My eyes were filled with tears, my little body shook, and my stomach began to heave. Not painfully, like nausea, but powerfully like adrenaline. Soon, my mouth began to utter noises, and words began to fill my mouth.

He that believeth on me, as the scripture hath said, out of his belly shall flow rivers of living water.

John 7:38 KJV

When a child receives the baptism in the Holy Spirit, there is an immediate download of purpose and responsibility. They are still children but children with understanding. When an adult receives the baptism of God's Spirit, there is an immediate sense of adventure, joy, and playfulness. When a child encounters God, the adult inside awakens. When an adult encounters God, the child inside awakens.

My nine-year-old experience was real, and I could not be convinced otherwise. What I took away from that experience was so unlike anything I had ever encountered. I felt like I was God's son. Not His "only begotten Son" but still His son. An overwhelming sense of security and purpose filled my life. I felt God's glory. The critic would say, "You're just a child," and that was true, so true that even to this day, I am just a child—a child of God.

"God is not looking for golden vessels, He is not even looking for silver vessels, He is looking for yielded vessels."

Kathryn Kuhlman

"The best ability is availability."

Doug Morgan

From that moment on, I have always felt under surveillance. I was acutely aware that God was watching over me. I have never felt alone. Even while living in disobedience, I have always felt the gentle nudge of God's Spirit urging me to surrender and to return. Even when my sin would take me far, His grace would go farther still. His rerouting has always been stronger than His rebuke. His favor has always prevailed over His fierce anger. His forgiveness has always been greater than my sin.

If we are faithless, he remains faithful, for he cannot disown himself.

2 TIMOTHY 2:13 NIV

Not that I have already obtained all this, or have already arrived at my goal, but I press on to take hold of that for which Christ Jesus took hold of me.

PHILIPPIANS 3:12 NIV

Although my personal experience was real and wonderful, we cannot interpret Scripture by our experiences. We interpret experience by Scripture. God's word is alive and true, and no experience can trump that. His word is settled in our hearts throughout eternity.

STEPHEN'S SECRET

Stephen is referred to as the first Christian martyr. His job may have seemed menial and unimportant. He was in charge of taking care of widows and the less fortunate. He specialized in running errands, cleaning up messes, creating menus, and providing meals. As an entry-level disciple, something was unique about Stephen. He was a courier with a powerful message, but until his time came, he would be faithful in the small things. He may have thought that his impact was private, but soon it would become very public.

But Stephen, full of the Holy Spirit, looked up to heaven and saw the glory of God, and Jesus standing at the right hand of God.

ACTS 7:55 NIV

Stephen's secret was a powerful relationship with the Holy Spirit. Except for the Sermon on the Mount, Stephen's discourse at his defense is the longest recorded sermon in the Bible. A man that waited tables has the second longest spoken message in the Bible — that is amazing!

In his speech, he describes with emotion who Israel is and where the nation is heading. His fearless and incriminating words pierce the hearts of his accusers saying, "Like your fathers...you do always resist the Holy Ghost." The Holy Spirit empowers us to have no fear while facing our adversaries.

The narrative of the martyrdom of Stephen is the only account of Jesus standing, not seated, at the Father's right hand. When you go all out for God, He will go all out for you. Of course, we totally rely on the Spirit's help. But the message of the Spirit is not dependency but empowerment. He empowers us to do what we could not do.

> *When you go all out for God, He will go all out for you.*

OCCUPY IDENTITY

So many are perpetually in search of this enigma we call identity. There is a mystery called "me." Without the guidance of the Holy Spirit, it is virtually impossible to find my true self, no matter how thoroughly

Supernatural Power on Earth

I search. Until I gather, accept, and receive confirmation on the "me data," I will continually look to others to validate or assign my identity. The end result is dissatisfaction and discouragement.

Being who God created is not easy; insecurities weigh heavily on authenticity. The apprehension is fear of rejection. If our true identity is rejected, we have nothing to fall back on—at least that's the lie we believe.

In reality, your real self is your best self. The easiest person to be is yourself. It is so uncomfortable to live the disingenuous life. We torment ourselves by seeking approval from others, when God confirms through His Spirt, "You're the one I want."

> We torment ourselves by seeking approval from others, when God confirms through His Spirt, "You're the one I want."

Perfection does not exist. It is not factual, and it is definitely not feasible. You will find more acceptance and appreciation for your flaws than for your fiction. Jesus declared that His Kingdom is within you. Therefore, your internal reality becomes your external reality. So how is the Kingdom? It may sound cliché, but how are you doing? The beauty is that God uses imperfect people to perform His perfect will on the earth. You were created with great purpose on the inside of you.

When we believe, we belong. Our faith is not frustrated by comparison but motivated even by others' accomplishments. When you occupy your identity, you have a base to grow from. The greatest room in the world is the room for improvement. We cannot afford to shrink in to doubt. We cannot afford self-loathing. This is contrary to God's plan. The Holy Spirit refuses to allow us to look down upon ourselves. This is not humility, this is deception—we are God's offspring.

BETWEEN A ROCK AND A HARD PLACE

One of the most colorful personalities around Jesus was His disciple Peter. Peter would fight at the drop of a hat, and he would drop the hat. Peter was highly opinionated and appeared to get temperamental occasionally. He is known for his impetuous, knee-jerk response at any given opportunity.

Peter's name means "rock." According to his name, he should be a reliable, stable, uncompromising force. Unfortunately, Peter has an archenemy — his name is Peter. No one is more destructive to Peter's life than Peter. Peter is not only the rock, he is the hard place.

Peter is torn by inconsistencies. He projected strength but often displayed weakness. Loud, boisterous, and obnoxious—no one wanted to cross Peter. On the outside he was fearless; on the inside he was weak. If you follow his words and actions, his life speaks of one thing: self-preservation. As Jesus is arrested and led away, Peter sheepishly follows behind, lurking in the shadows. Eventually, he's confronted by a young maid. As she discloses his identity, he immediately goes into a cussing tirade. Trying his best to distance himself from Jesus, he denies his Lord.

Now fifty days after the crucifixion, something life altering happens to Peter — he receives the baptism of the Holy Ghost. The Spirit is the agent of identity. A new man emerges. This man was in him before, undisclosed and lying dormant. On the day of Pentecost, the coward becomes a champion. There is absolutely no trace of fear. He has been delivered from fear and the expectations of others. He is strong, he is composed, he is uncompromising, yet well-behaved. He is not rattled. Transformed from a man that denied Christ, he is now the authoritative voice for the church.

The Holy Spirit is not the finishing touch; He is the final touch. Peter has been transformed. His transformation was immediate. It was not a reaction but a response. Peter will never be the same. The Holy Spirit has surfaced the new man; the man he was always meant to be. He no longer lives for Peter; he lives for Christ.

> The Holy Spirit is not the finishing touch; He is the final touch.

This transformation is more than modified behavior; Peter's true identity has finally been uncovered via Holy Spirit. The new, improved Peter knows no limits or boundaries. He is truly fearless. He is now a "rock" that Christ's church can be built upon.

Now it's Peter's turn to be led away. No longer hiding in obscurity, he's in the forefront. His ignominious death awaits — crucifixion is imminent. Traditionally, as the malefactor hangs suspended between Heaven and Earth, his lungs can no longer receive air. Death by crucifixion results in asphyxiation. As Peter is marched to his own execution, he is granted one request: "Flip the cross." His request was not for comfort or a speedy death. No, his request was made in honor of Christ's sacrifice. Peter's last wish would actually decelerate the rate of his own crucifixion. In death, he would be a living illustration of his own unworthiness to die like his Lord. Peter's last sermon would not be vocal but visual; his last opportunity to worship would be himself fastened to a cross upside down.

Peter's choice of execution was actually more tormenting, more time consuming, and more humiliating. Wow, what a statement! His last message was that of unworthiness—"Not worthy to die like my Lord." An iconic death for a man who turned the world upside down. He views the world as it truly is — upside down.

You're Grounded

But the Advocate, the Holy Spirit, whom the Father will send in my name, will teach you all things and will remind you of everything I have said to you.

JOHN 14:26

On November 20, 2013, a Boeing 747 cargo freighter inadvertently landed at Colonel James Jabara Airport, Wichita, Kansas*. The 747, which is the largest cargo plane, was destined for McConnell Air Force Base but got slightly off course. Colonel James Jabara Airport is a small general aviation airport, significantly smaller than the intended Air Force base. The smaller airport was actually on the same coordinates, just nine miles apart. Even though they were flying in the right direction of their destination, they came up short. In fact, the tiny airport runway falls 3000 ft short of what's necessary for liftoff. (**Fox News*, November 21, 2013. Accessed May 1, 2018. http://www.foxnews.com/us/2013/11/21/boeing-747-mistakenly-lands-at-small-kansas-airport.html.)

The name of the Boeing 747 is "Dream Lifter." Today's dreams are tomorrow's reality. Many dreams have been stranded, destined for greatness only to fall short. Maybe you have landed in an unsuitable place, an unsuitable job, or an unsuitable relationship. It's difficult to daily face the inner pressure of knowing you could fly but never having the ability to get off the tarmac. There's nothing more frustrating than being permanently grounded.

Every great dream begins with a dreamer. Always remember, you have within you the strength, the patience, and the passion to reach the stars to change the world.

Commonly attributed to Harriet Tubman, former slave, Civil War soldier and abolitionist

When our fears and failures have the upper hand, we lose hope and our dreams are denied. The worst grade I ever received was not a D or an F, but an Incomplete. Unfulfilled dreams create extremely bitter people. Without the ability to complete a task, our hopes lie in ruin.

Hope deferred makes the heart sick, but a longing fulfilled is a tree of life.

Proverbs 13:12 NIV

On a clear Monday evening, January 13, 2014, Southwest flight 4013 landed at Graham Clark Downtown Airport*. This also is a small municipal airport not designed for larger commercial planes. Carrying 124 passengers and 5 crewmembers, the airline had mistakenly landed at the wrong airport in Branson, Missouri. What's supposedly a vacation destination now becomes a holding cell of desperation. (*Associated Press*, January 13, 2014. Accessed April 30, 2018. https://www.yahoo.com/news/southwest-flight-lands-wrong-mo-airport-051057120.html.)

The average airport runway for a commercial flight is 7100 ft. long, while the runway in Branson was only 3700 ft long - without hard braking, significantly too short to land. And way too short for departure. Once again, another big dream grounded.

The unexpected arrival was due to pilot error; reportedly for flying "visually." Because of the uncommonly clear weather, there was no use for the aid of the autopilot. The copilot just went along for the ride.

Leave them; they are blind guides. If the blind lead the blind, both will fall into a pit.

MATTHEW 15:14 NIV

But you are not like that, for the Holy One has given you his Spirit, and all of you know the truth.

1 JOHN 2:20 NIV

The Holy Spirit provides answers from another world. From the vantage point of truth, we are not easily fooled. As children of God we don't look inward for identity, we look upward.

Whether we have willingly walked away from God, fallen prey to evils beyond our control, or totally miscalculated our direction in life, at some time or another we have all needed the Spirit's aid in course correction. We are lost without Him. Three men are on a boat 50 miles from shore. One of these men can't swim, another can swim about five miles, but one is an exceptional athlete. He can swim 35 miles. If the boat goes down, they are all in the same fatal predicament. When it all pans out, our effort and our abilities all come short of safety. We need not compare. We are hopeless without God. We are of all men most miserable.

> *All roads do not lead to God; the good news is, God can be found on every road.*

Secular spirituality would tell you that all roads lead to God. It is a lie, a damnable lie! All roads do not lead to God; the good news is, God can be found on every road.

This is why it is imperative to seek God, to learn of Him, to listen and obey. As we walk in obedience towards God, our identity becomes securely fixed and our purpose becomes clearly defined. But, even more important than that, our purpose is accomplished.

Identity is not defined by our possession but by our position in God.

Chapter 7

POWER ON
KNOWLEDGE, WISDOM, & DISCERNMENT

So that you are not lacking in any gift, awaiting eagerly the revelation of our Lord Jesus Christ...

1 Corinthians 1:7 NASB

MANY GIFTS, DIVINE IN NATURE

God has given many gifts through His Spirit that the mission of the church and the believer may be fulfilled. Gifts are divine in nature. All of the gifts are gifts of grace. All of the gifts are subject to the rule of love. Gifts are to be used, not abused. Everything that is said or done must be done out of love, for that is the nature of God's Spirit.

The gifts of the Spirit are not given as a reward but a responsibility. Gifts are for the common good, not for self-centered promotion. They are not given to launch selfish ambition but to draw the Body closer to God. They are bestowed for completion, not competition.

Supernatural Power on Earth

WHEN TWO PROPHETS MEET
("SPIRITUAL" ONE-UPMANSHIP)

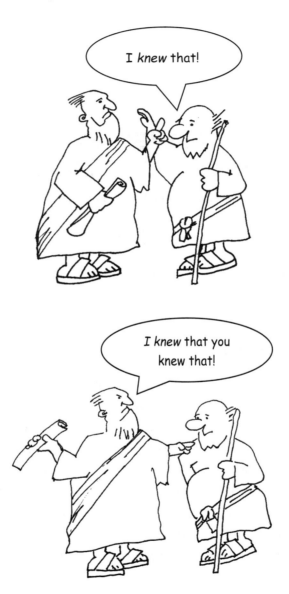

Spiritual gifts are not for status but for service. Rather, they establish, build up, and promote the Kingdom of God.

"The gifts of the Spirit are not badges of honor, but tools for the job assigned."

EVANGELIST REINHARD BONNKE,
TAKING ACTION: RECEIVING AND OPERATING IN THE GIFTS AND POWER OF THE HOLY SPIRIT, CHARISMA HOUSE, 2012

In the following scripture quotation, we have a list of supernatural gifts bestowed upon the church. These nine spiritual gifts (charism) are endowments, supernatural graces given by the Holy Spirit. These gifts are simply the ability to do what God has called us to do.

Now to each one the manifestation of the Spirit is given for the common good. To one there is given through the Spirit a message of wisdom, to another a message of knowledge by means of the same Spirit, to another faith by the same Spirit, to another gifts of healing by that one Spirit, to another miraculous powers, to another prophecy, to another distinguishing between spirits, to another speaking in different kinds of tongues, and to still another the interpretation of tongues.

1 CORINTHIANS 12:7-10 NIV

RELEVANCE

Which gift is most important? Though all gifts come from the same Spirit, they each have a distinct function. The most important gift is the one needed at the moment.

The apostle Paul uses the allegory of body parts to illustrate differences in function found within the same body; therefore, there is no competing within ourselves. Each gift is equally valid, but not equally valuable. For example, a toe, which is very important for balance, is not as valuable as an eye for reading. Necessity is what defines value. So the most important gift is the one needed at the moment. Value is estimated by the current need.

> The most important gift is the one needed at the moment.

Because these gifts were given to the body of Christ, we never want to be negligent in our operation of them all. They are vital to the spiritual health of the individual and body as a whole. They help us individually and help us to help others. They are for the common good.

There is usually a gift an individual is attracted to. What gift are you most interested in? Which gift has ministered to you the most? These questions help to define what gifting the Holy Spirit is leading us towards. You will find that as you yield yourself to these giftings, you will instinctively begin to respond to at least one of the nine gifts.

NINE GIFTS OF THE SPIRIT

The nine gifts are easily classified into three categories of three. Many divide these categories in the same way, but the category labels are often different. This is not doctrinal; the categories serve only as a tool for memory and function.

1. Revelation gifts
   - Word of wisdom
   - Word of knowledge
   - Discerning of spirits

2. Power gifts
   - Faith
   - Gifts of healing
   - Working of miracles

3. Vocal gifts
   - Prophecy
   - Tongues
   - Interpretation of tongues

The apostle Paul desires to impart these gifts that had been entrusted unto him. Therefore, we can understand that spiritual gifts are given to be given.

> *I long to see you so that I may impart to you some spiritual gift to make you strong…*
>
> ROMANS 1:11 NIV

Gifts are to be desired and developed. Spiritual gifts will strengthen the recipient, so that they may strengthen others. All benefit when the supernatural gifts of the Spirit are in operation.

> *Now eagerly desire the greater gifts…*
>
> 1 CORINTHIANS 12:31 NIV

THE WORD OF WISDOM

The word of wisdom is the supernatural application of knowledge in a particular situation. This is often demonstrated through divine direction in a given circumstance. Simply put, the word of wisdom is actually the Holy Spirit thinking through a person. This knowledge helps us know how to move forward in a course of action. It helps us to rightfully determine, decide, and know what to do at a given moment.

> *Your ears will hear a word behind you, "This is the way, walk in it," whenever you turn to the right or to the left.*
>
> ISAIAH 30:21 NASB

Wisdom often works in conjunction with the gift of knowledge. Knowledge is the accumulation of facts, while wisdom is the assessment and understanding of the data. Wisdom recognizes and analyzes the situation then weighs in with advice of which you would otherwise be oblivious.

Wisdom is the divine problem solver. Wisdom is the house built with the storm in mind. Through this special gift, we are able to make right decisions and avoid regret. When we fail to acknowledge this gift, we often find ourselves subject to cyclical patterns of failure.

Have you ever noticed that the wisest in the room never draw attention to themselves? They seem so content and confident. This is a result of godly wisdom. They are not prideful; they just have a different spirit. They are poised and unwavering, sensitive but not emotional. Wisdom offers a self-sustaining confidence.

The purposes of a person's heart are deep waters, but one who has insight draws them out.

PROVERBS 20:5 NIV

Wisdom knows how to hold its peace and is content to surface at a later time. Wisdom does not feel the need to always make its case but will always make a difference.

Sadly, we are prone to be manipulated by popular opinion. Wisdom isn't always popular.

"If I am pleasing to God I may be rejected by men, if I am pleasing to men, I may be rejected by God."

LEONARD RAVENHILL

Chaos is the reward for people who do not walk in godly wisdom. True wisdom is to know the best course of action and to follow through by doing it, whether people are in agreement with it or not. The sons of Issachar were just such men—devout men of understanding, who knew what to do in their days (1 Chronicles 12:32). They were in tune with God's wisdom for their times and were able to preserve Israel from destruction.

The Dreamer's Secret

An example in Scripture of a man who walked in godly wisdom is found in the life of Joseph. Joseph's life was an illustrated truth. Through dreams of his own or of others, he instinctively knew what must be done. In fact, Genesis 39:22 says, "Whatever needed to be done, he was the doer of it." Wisdom defined his life as he listened and obeyed. Through wisdom, Joseph not only prevailed as an individual but established polices for distribution of food before a potentially devastating global famine. During difficult days, his wisdom would ensure the preservation of the Jews, from whose posterity Christ would be born. Therefore, we are all the beneficiaries of Joseph's wisdom. What could have been starvation resulted in salvation.

A Bad Dream becomes Reality

For a number of years, my father-in-law and I bred horses. I once dreamed that my mare and its colt were in dire trouble. In my dream, I saw the horse with its foal. The mare stood helplessly as the colt lay lifeless on the barn floor. In the dream, I jumped over the stall and began to administer help and warmth to the unresponsive colt. I briskly rubbed the colt's chest, back, and neck, working frantically to revive him. Suddenly, he began to respond. A short but disturbing dream.

Though the dream was brief, I felt I had also been given the interpretation. I felt the Holy Spirit was speaking to me about our new church plant. We had recently birthed a new church out of our existing church. Of course, every work can be demanding, but this work in particular had been under a litany of attacks. There had been splits and divisions, and there were unsubstantiated lawsuits from a harassing denomination. Inundated with so much confusion, I was baffled at what to do next and desperate to find true north. The dream, though not giving specifics, encouraged me to stay with it. Don't let death win; actively engage in the process even if it looks futile. Even in crisis, you can be encouraged if you know you're being led by a higher power.

The dream gave unique perspective in dealing with the myriad of difficulties. I knew that this "young colt" full of potential would need special hands-on attention. It would not be something that I could do through vision alone; this would require personal contact. I had been operating under a great amount of pressure, as if to keep my head above the water. Being a church planter with a proclivity towards risk, I had been there before. This was so much more — this was an uncommon burden, so the Holy Spirit gave uncommon warning. Beyond feeling the warning, God wanted me to feel the reality.

Some dreams lie dormant until triggered, then they are extremely lucid and easily recalled. The next morning as I started my day, I rushed out of the house and quickly backed out of the driveway. Then I stopped—something said, "Wait." Immediately I recalled the strange dream.

This is that moment. The moment you inconvenience yourself with a response or later agonize with a regret. Some never miss an opportunity to miss an opportunity. I thought to myself, "What can it hurt to check?" So instead of leaving, I drove my truck right into the barn as if there was an emergency. After all, I was busy that morning.

Surreal, just like the dream, the mare was standing over the lifeless colt. This was not *déjà vu*; this was for real. Could I be living out this dream in real time?

I could see that as the colt had laid down to rest its legs had been trapped in the stall gate. It was easy to investigate — the colt had thrashed the ground all night. Deep depressions in the earthen barn floor gave all the evidence needed. The more the colt tried to escape, the more it wedged itself into the gate. The mare could only stand helplessly by, unable to deliver the now-exhausted colt.

I jumped the gate, stepped beside the helpless mother, and pulled the colt from under the gate and with both hands vigorously rubbed the colt's neck, back, and chest. After a few moments, he revived and was back on his feet. Eminent death had been avoided.

So was the Holy Spirit trying to save the colt or the church? The answer was, "YES!"

We are encouraged in James 1:5 to ask for wisdom. It is God's desire to give us wisdom. Knowledge brings awareness and recognition; wisdom lets us know what to do next.

But the wisdom that comes from heaven is first of all pure; then peace-loving, considerate, submissive, full of mercy and good fruit, impartial and sincere.

JAMES 3:17 NIV

The gift of wisdom is not the common wisdom that God has promised every believer. This gift is designed for dilemma. This gift thrives in times of trial by precise application. It searches out and finds the secret formula that unlocks mysteries and secures divine direction.

THE WORD OF KNOWLEDGE

The word of knowledge is the in-depth understanding of a particular issue. Again, this is supernatural intel. Through this word or impression, the Holy Spirit gives knowledge we would not otherwise have — it is internal, spiritual knowledge. The Holy Spirit downloads revelation concerning the past, present, or future. This could be a single word, a feeling, or simply an inner knowing.

> *A word of knowledge is simply a powerful fragment of the knowledge of God.*

A word is a fragment of a sentence. So, a word of knowledge is simply a powerful fragment of the knowledge of God. It is the essence and power of the whole, made simple for human interaction.

Spiritual Dashboard

The gifts of revelation act as a divine dashboard to help us navigate life. They warn, assure, and protect us as we move through hostile terrain. They provide the supernatural clarity to advance with surety.

Words of knowledge usually have more shock value to the hearer than words of wisdom. When a word of knowledge is spoken, there is often a "wow factor" involved because the knowledge is supernatural and known only to the hearer. The recipient has an immediate emotional attachment to the words given, because the facts can be immediately validated. The word is authenticated when it is understood that this is supernatural, divine knowledge not naturally known by the speaker. This gives credibility to what may come next.

On the other hand, words of wisdom are not always readily celebrated because they may encourage someone to do what they do not desire to do. Wisdom may be rejected because of mental filters or pride. They sometimes demand a response that is undesirable to the recipient of the word.

While words of knowledge may have shock value, words of wisdom have navigational value in the ultimate pursuit of a preferred outcome.

Albert Einstein said, "The only source of knowledge is experience." (*Ideas And Opinions*, Crown Publishing Group, p. 271.) I am sure Albert was sincere, but he was sincerely wrong. Although common knowledge is acquired through experience, uncommon knowledge that comes from the Holy Spirit can take an inexperienced novice and promote him to a place that even the experienced must recognize.

THE POWER OF OBEDIENCE

Agabus, a prophet who lived in Jerusalem, had no training in meteorology and had probably never travelled extensively. But when the Spirit spoke to him, he listened. He was also faithful to report what he observed in the Spirit. We often miss this point and find ourselves later thinking, "I knew that."

Knowledge for knowledge's sake has no value; it is worthless. Knowledge alone can make one proud and miserable. You've heard it said, "Nobody likes a know-it-all." Knowledge must be acted upon in order to find its redeeming quality.

> *During this time some prophets came down from Jerusalem to Antioch. One of them, named Agabus, stood up and through the Spirit predicted that a severe famine would spread over the entire Roman world. (This happened during the reign of Claudius.) The disciples, as each one was able, decided to provide help for the brothers and sisters living in Judea.*
>
> ACTS 11:27- 29 NIV

Agabus predicted a severe famine and with this prophetic insight the disciples would be equipped to know and go. Acting upon the prophetic word was critical to the saving of lives. Time-sensitive knowledge must be acted upon immediately.

Many have avoided the prophetic because they feel they have insufficient knowledge. They don't want to do something crazy because of a hunch. They want to be more informed. We have been conditioned for mediocrity. The last thing we want to do is stand out.

The need for reliability and accuracy has sometimes prevented a timely prophetic word from surfacing. There is a fine line between daring faith and reckless enthusiasm. I try to vet words of prophecy through personal criteria of motive. If it brings only God glory, I usually go with it. The Bible says that at best we only see in part so we prophesy in part. Knowing this helps alleviate the pressure of performance. We are God's workmanship, so we push for progress, not perfection.

WARNING AND PROTECTION

Many recall the first strike of the Gulf War in the nineties. I remember watching the black and white footage retrieved from our warplanes as they bombed strategic targets in massive air campaigns. It was amazing to view the devastation from that vantage point. It was as if we were fighting together. Although not available in technicolor, these videos of actual war were impressively haunting.

Years later, I was traveling on Interstate 75 in Dayton, Ohio. The drive was extremely congested as I navigated my way through the hectic work-hour traffic. Suddenly, a curious shift took place in my spirit. It was so bazaar — it was as if time stood still. The traffic that was so heavily congested mysteriously began to separate. Strangely, two packs of cars were formed from the one, and I was left alone in the middle. The traffic was heavy one hundred yards in front of me; the traffic was equally crowded one hundred yards behind me.

Then, as a solitary car on the interstate, my mind began to drift. I saw that black and white footage from Desert Storm. I imagined myself being the target in a massive air campaign. So bazaar but so profound. Instinctively, I grabbed the wheel with both hands. I was undeniably feeling this moment. But, why?

Then it happened. As I drove under an overpass what appeared to be a mass of ribbon fell in front of my truck. Hands still securely holding the wheel in 10/2 position, I sped over the obstruction that had just missed my hood. Under my seat, fireworks began to pop. The blur that fell from the sky turned out to be strings of fireworks.

I must confess, that I'm guilty of having fun at others expense. Some may even call this karma, but this was an irresponsible practical joke. While I've always enjoyed jokes, this was dangerous. If I had not been alerted by the Spirit, I don't know what would have happened. Even on guard, the noise was startling.

I'm sure these were just young kids were having fun at a helpless commuter's expense. It may have been just for fun, but something that startling could have been life-threatening. I'll never forget it because I know I was warned by the Spirit.

PRAYER ADVANCE

My parents had taken my younger brother with them to a ministry gathering in New Orleans. Of course, what could go wrong in New Orleans? My little brother Luke and three friends were hanging out. Two guys, two girls just having fun, painting the town red. Around midnight, they were walking down Canal Street and their peaceful evening of sight-seeing was interrupted by gunfire. Stunned and terrified, they found themselves in the middle of a drive-by shooting. The four surprised teens ducked behind a parked car for safety. They were safe, but the car beside them was shot several times. Shook up, they immediately hailed a cab and went back to their hotel rooms.

When Luke entered the hotel room, my father got up from his knees and asked, "What happened? The Holy Ghost woke your mother and

I up." They were both interceding for the four teens, two of which are now full-time ministers. This is a clear-cut example of how the spirit realm works. While the unsuspecting teens were thrust into harm's way, the Holy Spirit sent an impression to my dad to do the only thing he could do—pray!

DISCERNING OF SPIRITS

Discernment detects the source of information, whether it is of God or of Satan. It allows us to know internally what is right or wrong; it is a supernatural revelation of the Holy Spirit, distinct from natural, human reasoning. Through discerning of spirits, the Spirit communicates by using impressions, mental images, warnings and sensory methods. By this gift, also often called distinguishing of spirits, the nebulous becomes obvious.

> *By discernment, or distinguishing of spirits, the nebulous becomes obvious.*

Some things may even be good but not good for *me*.

> *"Discernment is not knowing the difference between right and wrong, discernment is knowing the difference between right and almost right."*
>
> CHARLES SPURGEON

When we are discerning spirits, there are three that we must keep in mind: the human spirit, the Holy Spirit, and evil or satanic spirits. Discernment helps us to detect false revelation, discern the plans of Satan, and discover the plans of God.

We are designed by God with a strong human spirit. We are amazed when we hear of survivors that have withstood extreme circumstances such as fire, water, or heights, only to miraculously survive. This tenacious will is due to our Creator, as He made us in His image. But human achievements or endeavors fall short of where God wants to lead us. He wants us to live in the supernatural realm.

Without the Spirit, we process data and make decisions based upon our human assessment, operating with limited, natural abilities. We need more. We need the Spirit to engage our beings for deeper understanding without the restrictions of natural, human capabilities.

For he is our God and we are the people of his pasture, the flock under his care. Today, if only you would hear his voice...
Psalms 95:7 NIV

Discernment helps us to judge well through divine perception. The obscure and enigmatic becomes clear and obvious. Ulterior motives are disclosed and evil intentions are thwarted through discernment. We can distinguish between what's gold and what's gold-plated.

Discernment is a gift of grace that must be subject to love. It is not the gift of suspicion. We prophecy in part but not in paranoia. This gift is never to be fear-based.

"A man who is intimate with God is not intimidated by man."
Leonard Ravenhill, *Why Revival Tarries*
Bethany House, August 1, 2004 (first published 1959)

Because of the nature of this gift, one can easily be labeled as judgmental. And those who truly are judgmental often hide behind their "gift" to express their agenda. If one operates in true discernment, they don't feel the need to say everything they know. They wait on God's timing and God's character. Discernment warns, protects, encourages, and restores. Without love, this gift is of no value.

Truth Is Not Proof

In Acts chapter 16, the Bible tells us of the street ministry of Paul and Silas. As they minister, a young girl follows behind them. She is confirming in every way. She never seeks to oppose them but validates and verifies every word they speak. She's the one shouting "Amen!" but before long they will be saying "Oh, me!" Discernment is extremely valuable because it helps to pinpoint how things *are* rather than how you *think they are*.

The girl is unknown to Paul and Silas but no stranger to this community. She has been a human tool for witchcraft and divination. Now she pulls along beside them with her approval. Her validation is not required — they are already validated by God's Spirit.

God also testified to it by signs, wonders and various miracles, and by gifts of the Holy Spirit distributed according to his will.

Hebrews 2: 4 NIV

The girl is using this opportunity to validate herself and the demons she hosts. She declares that these men are servants of the Most High God, and they are telling you the way to be saved. Although she's annoying, she's spot on. This is relevant and accurate information. Nevertheless, her announcements are not helping the mission but hindering it.

Day after day, she follows the ministry; she must be corrected. She is demon-possessed. The information may be accurate, but it is coming through an evil source. I've found that when it comes to demonic spirits, if you don't embarrass them, they will embarrass you.

Interesting twist — we don't always expect the truth to come from Satan. Therefore, truth is not proof! What? That's right, truth is not proof. According to 2 Corinthians 11:14, Satan himself masquerades as an angel of light. This is how most cults are formed. There is an element of truth that has veered off course over time. This is why doctrine is so important. This is why what someone *says* is not as important as what they *do*. Satan is a counterfeit. Satan can imitate anything except a holy lifestyle.

You know, we live with whatever we will tolerate. Without the gift of discernment, every voice speaking truth can be tolerated, whether from God or Satan. Unfortunately, what we tolerate, we deserve.

> *But solid food is for the mature, for those who have their powers of discernment trained by constant practice to distinguish good from evil.*
>
> Hebrews 5:14 ESV

Paul has finally heard enough. Direct confrontation is the necessary action for this spirit to be exposed and exorcised. Paul turned around and said to the spirit, "In the name of Jesus Christ I command you to come out of her!" At that moment, the spirit left her.

Misinformation attempts to stay in the same lane as accurate information. Then it slowly and gradually begins to change coordinates. Basically, you start right and end wrong. In the long run, the end is what matters.

DISCERNMENT HELPS US SEE MORE

> *Now when the attendant of the man of God had risen early and gone out, behold, an army with horses and chariots was circling the city. And his servant said to him, "Alas, my master! What shall we do?" So he answered, "Do not fear, for those who are with us are more than those who are with them." Then Elisha*

prayed and said, "O LORD, I pray, open his eyes that he may see." And the LORD opened the servant's eyes and he saw; and behold, the mountain was full of horses and chariots of fire all around Elisha.

2 Kings 6:15-17 NIV

Elisha was being pursued by the Syrian army. Their nighttime reconnaissance had paid off; during the night, the Syrians had pinpointed his whereabouts. They had completely surrounded him in Dothan - or so they thought. The Hebrew word *Dothan* means "law'.

It is time for you to act, LORD; your law is being broken.

Psalms 119:126 NIV

Elisha's servant wakes up surprised by the enemy's advance through the night. He is beside himself with fear and panic. The worst company you will ever keep is when you are beside yourself. Alarmed, he wakes up the prophet asking, "What do we do?"

Fear is debilitating. Fear operates from uncertainty, but is crippling when compounded by factual information.

The servant is clearly seeing the armies of their enemy cut them off from any chance of survival. He clearly sees their chariots, horses, and weaponry. The servant sees but doesn't see enough. Discernment helps us to see more. We can see crisis but sometimes lose sight of Christ. The servant has no problem with seeing, he just can't see enough.

"The only thing worse than being blind is having sight with no vision."

Helen Keller, *The Story of My Life*
Wilder Publications, October 24, 2012

Supernatural Power on Earth

Vision is released in the battle. Conflict reveals purpose more than any other criteria. Vision sees a preferred outcome in advance. Positive results are the result of a positive vision. Those who are pure in heart will see God in every situation (Matthew 5:8). God's favor pursues and protects His faithful.

By this I know that You are pleased with me, Because my enemy does not shout in triumph over me.

PSALM 41:11 NASB

Elisha's servant is given the opportunity to look again. He is granted the privilege of seeing more. The final verdict is "they that are with us are more than they that are against us."

A Guarding Impression

While in high school I met a man named Jimmy. We worked together in a department store stockroom. Jimmy was married with little children and they all seemed so nice. But as I look back in hindsight, there were definite signs of negligence towards his family.

Jimmy and I hit it off immediately and despite him being in his thirties, we both liked to work out so that gave us a lot in common. He invited me to his garage, which he had converted into a weight room. It seemed harmless; there were other football players that worked out there so my brother and I began to work out with Jimmy. About two weeks in to this new friendship, out of the blue my father told us to leave Jimmy alone. He asked me and my brother Jon not to go back to Jimmy's garage gym, so we didn't.

About a month later, Jimmy was arrested for stealing out of the stockroom. After he was released from jail, I began to notice his motorcycle at my high school. I believe Jimmy was selling drugs, although I have no proof of that.

Soon he began to date a girl in my senior class. Devastated, I would see him pull up to the high school and she would get on the back of his bike. A sad commentary of rebellion. I could only see his wife and children's faces in my head.

About six months after graduation, Jimmy stabbed the young girl he had been dating. She barely escaped with her life. And off to prison Jimmy went.

My dad was by no means an austere man; it actually seemed out of character for him to forbid my brother and I to shun anyone. He was never overprotective or strict, but when he said, "Leave him alone," he was saving us from who knows what. Discernment sees what the natural eyes dismiss.

The revelation gifts are to profit the common good. If you look for these gifts, they will come searching for you. They are activated when engaged. It has been said that you attract what you are attracted to.

Knowing the blessing of operating in these gifts, I urge you to taste and see. These supernatural charismas are given to profit us all. If the gift is of no profit, it is either being abused or out of alignment with God's timing. Don't allow the abuse of a gift to prevent you from desiring a gift. Ask the Holy Spirit for wisdom, knowledge, and discernment. These gifts are not earned, they are given but often presented by request. Ask and you shall receive.

Chapter 8

POWER ON
FAITH, HEALING, & MIRACLES

There are varieties of effects, but the same God who works all things in all persons. But to each one is given the manifestation of the Spirit for the common good.

1 Corinthians 12:6-7 NIV

Just as your body has organs to benefit the whole, the body of Christ is dependent upon special endowments for the health of the whole body. Some parts of your body have always been activated such as the respiratory system. Your lungs were activated at birth. Now, your legs, that's a different story. Although you had to learn to walk, you were always supposed to. Some gifts will require you to place a demand upon them. They may refuse to respond immediately; this is why we cannot abort a gift prematurely.

As with other gifts of the Spirit, this group of three, often referred to as "the power gifts," are used as a supernatural conduit to accomplish what God desires to do on Earth. They are tools used to accomplish God's plans. These special abilities are provided to the believer by the Spirit.

> God's graces and gifts are given to every believer, not only to those in fulltime ministry or to a select few.

God's graces and gifts are given to every believer, not only to those in fulltime ministry or to a select few. He doesn't limit His supernatural power to "clergy"; the division between the priesthood and laity has been removed in Christ, just as the dividing lines between Jew and Gentile, slave and free, men and women have been erased. All believers have been made priests unto God and should serve in the strength of His unlimited grace and power. (See Rev. 1:6; 5:10; 1 Pet. 2:9.) Paul explained this to the Corinthian church, as found in the passage below with emphasis on the aspect of **each believer's** spiritual ability to profit all.

*Now **to each one** the manifestation of the Spirit is given for the common good... All these are the work of one and the same Spirit, and he distributes them **to each one**, just as he determines [emphasis added].*

1 CORINTHIANS 12:7, 11 NIV

THE GIFT OF FAITH

There are three types of faith: saving faith, the fruit of faith, and the gift of faith.

Saving faith comes in measures. We have all been given a measure of faith. This faith is what enables all men to come to salvation in Christ. No one is excluded that calls Jesus Lord.

For through the grace given to me I say to everyone among you not to think more highly of himself than he ought to think; but to

think so as to have sound judgment, as God has allotted to each a measure of faith.

Romans 12:3 NASB

The fruit of faith is a key ingredient of the fruit of the Spirit. This fruit has been planted within us all by the Holy Spirit. We are known by our fruit. Therefore, fruit is imperative in spiritual identification. Gifts can come immediately but fruit takes time. Said another way, gifts are given but fruit is grown.

But the fruit of the Spirit is love, joy, peace, longsuffering, gentleness, goodness, faith, meekness, temperance.

Galatians 5:22-23a KJV

Then there is the gift of faith. The gift of faith is beyond the common faith God has given each believer. This gift is a supernatural ability to believe. It is a God-given ability that is not worked up by desire but by divine endowment. In fact, if you have this gift, it is hard *not* to believe. When operating in this gift, doubt becomes null and void. Circumstances, no matter how dire, become irrelevant.

> The gift of faith is a God-given ability that is not worked up by desire but by divine endowment.

The gift of faith is denoted by a divine certainty with no shadow of doubt. It is diametrically opposed to unbelief. When asked "Why?" this gift responds with "I know that I know!" While unbelief has a debilitating effect, this gift destroys doubt and encourages boldness.

This gift has an assignment. Like our SEAL Team 6, this gift has specific objectives, but fulfilment is often contingent upon timing and obedience.

The gift of faith enables us to trust God completely while encouraging others to do likewise. It is always beneficial to surround yourself with faith people.

This gift operates under a strong anointing. Spiritual atmospheres are important for this gift to be released. Because faith is the language of Heaven, Heaven takes notice when this gift is engaged. Faith honors God and God honors faith.

Faith Triggers

There were times in the early days of church planting that I felt discouraged to the point I considered a career change. I needed the Holy Spirit's encouragement because my resolve was beginning to weaken.

During a Wednesday night service, I felt to push through my doubts and just rely on God. As I was preaching, something was stirring inside of me.

Around twenty faithful people were in attendance — we had very humble beginnings. As I ministered faith began to rise. This has always been difficult to explain, but once you experience this kind of faith you understand. It's as if adrenaline has been released throughout your body and doubt is extinct. I call this a powerful, peaceful, profound place.

Again, nothing extraordinary was happening that the small congregation could outwardly see, but inside of me, a tsunami of faith was rising. Before a tsunami hits landfall, there is a great recession. It's been reported that on some shores the water can recede hundreds of yards.

As I came to my benediction, I received a word of knowledge from the Holy Spirit. I said, "There will come a day when people will enter this church and without hesitation or reservation walk straight to this pulpit and say, 'I want to be saved.'" I then closed in prayer.

As the people began to gather their belongings, the back door swung open. A distraught young mother with a baby in a blanket walked straight down the aisle. Everyone noticed her because she had completely missed the service. She stood in front of the pulpit crying and with a soft voice said, "I want to be saved." OMG!

We went through the sinner's prayer together; she then held out her baby—a beautiful, dark-haired baby girl.

"The doctors have told me she has cerebral palsy," the mother said. Undone, she added, "She will never walk or use her hands…"

I, on the other hand, had just witnessed the prophetic word instantaneously become reality. My faith was alive! Without patience or thought, throwing reason to the side, I spoke over the mother declaring, "No, she will walk, talk, and function as a normal child!" I could not be convinced otherwise. This is the gift of faith. Bottom line — knowing!

> *Faith has an epicenter. It is where the core belief gets stronger than the outside resistance.*

The mother was not a part of our congregation and I was told she had moved to another city shortly after. Needless to say, we lost touch with her.

Around fifteen years later, I had just opened a new church location about an hour's drive from our central location. At the close of a service, a beautiful, young, dark-haired teenaged girl stood before me. She asked, "Do you remember me?" A little embarrassed, I said, "I'm sorry, no, who are you?"

She said, "I'm the baby you prayed for!" There before me stood the picture of health, the precious child, fully grown — a direct result of the gift of faith.

Faith has an epicenter. It is where the core belief gets stronger than the outside resistance. Eventually, the outer doubt must accommodate the overwhelming, inner presence of faith. So, from the center to the circumference we begin to see faith grow. This is that unique, miraculous place where private becomes public, where doubt will be robbed and faith will rise, where what you have known in your spirit becomes a reality acknowledged by all. This is where the test becomes the testimony.

THE GIFTS OF HEALINGS

Note that "the gifts of healings" is plural, not singular (1 Cor. 12:9, 28, 30). This is because it applies to body, soul, and spirit. God's healing encompasses more than just physical healing; it includes emotional and mental healing as well. Our Father's compassion for the sick and broken goes deeper than physical healing alone — He wants us to be made whole in every area of our beings. Healing removes the affliction and restores what is broken.

This gift is extremely effective and cannot be attributed to the practice of medicine; it is straight from God. Neither is this gift explained by science, for it is miraculous, not a cure or a medical breakthrough. There is no certain formula or method pertaining to this gift. It is remarkable and always restorative. This gift validates the near presence of God and affirms the Holy Spirit's supernatural power to heal.

Healing may not come immediately when this gift is in operation; it may come gradually, as it did when the ten lepers met Jesus on the road. As they were walking it out, He was working it out. The working of miracles is usually an instantaneous occurrence, while gifts of healings can be immediate or gradual.

In Mark 16:15-19, Jesus commissioned the disciples, telling them to "Go into all the world and preach the gospel to all creation. Whoever believes and is baptized will be saved, but whoever does not believe will be condemned. And these signs will accompany those who believe...they will place their hands on sick people, and they will get well." Here we can see that all believers can pray for healing. In fact, this is our duty.

HEALING ALL MANNER OF DISEASE

Jesus operated in the gifts of healings as He healed all manner of disease.

> *[H]ow God anointed Jesus of Nazareth with the Holy Spirit and power, and how he went around doing good and healing all who were under the power of the devil, because God was with him.*
>
> ACTS 10:38 NIV

> *Jesus went throughout Galilee, teaching in their synagogues, proclaiming the good news of the kingdom, and healing every disease and sickness among the people.*
>
> MATTHEW 4:23 NIV

> *Jesus went through all the towns and villages, teaching in their synagogues, proclaiming the good news of the kingdom and healing every disease and sickness.*
>
> MATTHEW 9:35 NIV

He then gave this power to heal all manner of disease to His followers:

> *And when he had called unto him his twelve disciples, he gave them power against unclean spirits, to cast them out, and to heal all manner of sickness and all manner of disease.*
>
> MATTHEW 10:1 KJV

Supernatural Power on Earth

I have personally laid hands on hundreds of people and have experienced the healing power of God myself. In our ministry, we have seen almost every disease you can imagine healed, including cancer and AIDS. I believe in healing!

Therefore confess your sins to each other and pray for each other so that you may be healed. The prayer of a righteous person is powerful and effective.

JAMES 5:16 NIV

When I pray for someone's healing, I place a demand on the blood of Jesus. I ask the Father to remember His Son's back. The stripes on Jesus' back are a reference point for the believer.

Who Himself bore our sins in His own body on the tree, that we, having died to sins, might live for righteousness—by whose stripes you were healed.

1 PETER 2:24 NKJV

THE SPIRIT'S GIFTS ARE NOT SELF-CENTRIC

As with all the Holy Spirit's graces, the gift of healing is not self-centric. It is not limited to personal use; it goes beyond you. It is not exclusive but inclusive. This gift serves the body; obviously, it is a gift to be given. Received from the Holy Spirit, the gifts of healings are presented inwardly but practiced outwardly. As they are imparted by the Spirit, it is vital for the body that they be utilized.

It is possible to reject the precious gift that you have been entrusted with, but you will be robbing yourself of personal potential, followed by the disappointment of missed opportunity. Even more critical, if you fail to stir up this gift, you rob others. In the case of healing, this could be life-threatening. Inaction is not an option. Failing to engage in your gift is unacceptable and, quite honestly, unsustainable for a believer. I'm not intending to be judgmental, and this may sound harsh, but it would be a shame if someone remained infirm because you refused to be obedient to the Spirit. It may even be considered a sin of omission.

> *The gift of healing is not self-centric, not limited to personal use. This gift serves the body; obviously, it is a gift to be given.*

If anyone, then, knows the good they ought to do and doesn't do it, it is sin for them.

JAMES 4:17 NIV

HEALING FOR THOSE WHO BELIEVE

According to Scripture, there is only one criteria for a miracle. Only believe — all things are possible to those who believe. Faith honors God, and God honors faith in return.

Healing is referred to as the children's (believer's) bread (that which sustains and strengthens us). We can lay hands on the sick, we can anoint with oil, and we can expect healing; it has been promised to the Christian. My parents raised five children, four of which are boys. There wasn't a week

> *We can lay hands on the sick, we can anoint with oil, and we can expect healing; it has been promised to the Christian.*

that went by that someone wasn't hurt. Raising four rambunctious boys kept my mother busy applying mercurochrome and Band-Aids. She practically painted us orange. At times, our home looked like a triage unit. Nevertheless, my parents totally relied on the healing power of Jesus. My parents would go to the anointing oil long before they would grab the insurance card. I am thankful for my faith history.

In 1973 I was seven years old when my grandfather, Archie Luke, who pastored a church in Cramerton, North Carolina, began to show signs of a serious illness. He experienced severe headaches and thought he had become ill with a sinus infection. His temperature began to spike, and he felt feverish for days.

He went to the doctor who prescribed medication for what he thought was a viral infection. Pappa (Archie) got worse. Unable to sit up, he became nauseous and complained that even his teeth hurt, like the pain of an abscess. He went to bed and slept for an unusually long time. When my grandmother tried to wake him, she discovered he was unconscious. He was rushed to Gaston County Memorial Hospital where he was put in isolation. He remained unconscious with a temperature of 106 degrees and was placed in cold water to combat the fever. Believed to have meningitis, he was put through a battery of tests.

A flood of prayers from the people he pastored and from all over the world was lifted up for him. Preparing for the worst, the family was called in.

I am particularly fond of my Aunt Janet's experience during this traumatic event. She and her husband Bob flew in to North Carolina from Ohio. While in transit, she recalled asking God for a sign. She was open to God's will for her father but needed a sign to confirm it.

When they arrived at the hospital, they were allowed to quickly go to Pappa's bedside. Suited in protective gear, they could only look on as he floated in water with I.V.'s hanging all around. Janet asked to touch her father and was told she could not, which struck a sensitive chord within her spirit. She said within herself, "Maybe I can't touch my earthly father, but I can surely touch my heavenly Father." Then she did what we do — she prayed in the Spirit.

Ashen in color, seemingly frozen with illness, Archie's eyes slowly opened. "Hey, pretty," he said to Janet. Then he looked at Bob and said, "How you walkin', Brother Bob? By faith?" This was Janet's sign. Faith!

Without courageous faith, it is impossible to please God (Hebrews 11:6); we insult God with anemic faith. We play it safe, to stay in control. This position does not protect God from failure; in our minds, it relieves us of disappointment. Faith opposes and offends the natural mind. Faith moves the heart of God.

The lead doctor left for the night, after he preemptively signed a death certificate for my grandfather. This would prove to be premature. In fact, my grandfather still had churches to plant and pastor before his time to leave Earth would come. Thirty-five years later, my grandfather would receive his second death certificate. This would also be inaccurate because he has graduated from death unto life eternal!

"Someday you will read in the papers that D.L. Moody is dead, don't you believe a word of it! At that moment I shall be more alive than I am now."

DWIGHT L. MOODY, AMERICAN EVANGELIST

ALL BELIEVERS MAY PRAY HEALING PRAYER

All believers may lay hands and pray for healing, expecting to see it manifest as the result of petitioning God on behalf of the sick. Jesus has commissioned His followers to pray for the sick in His Name — as His Body, we are now His hands, feet, and voice. Believers are the channel of His supernatural power on Earth.

Healing may come as an answer to individual or group prayer or as the sick are anointed by the church elders who pray the prayer of faith (James 5:15). Regardless of the way healing comes, it is a divine enablement, a specialized anointing for a specific purpose. It is a special endowment that you did not earn through education or application. It is supernatural power given by the Holy Spirit.

I believe in healing. But not everyone is healed as we suppose they should be. I don't understand why, as I have seen many healed and many not healed. Rather than become a skeptic, I surrender my will to God's will. I don't accept failure for not having enough faith, and I don't agree with those who place that kind of pressure on those hurting. God is not forced or manipulated into action. The Scripture is replete with examples of healing with strong faith or with little faith. When we don't understand "why," we rely on the sovereignty of God. According to Hebrews 11, relying on God with no apparent results is not evidence of lack of faith; rather, it's the framework of faith.

One day Jesus was teaching, and Pharisees and teachers of the law were sitting there. They had come from every village of Galilee and from Judea and Jerusalem. And the power of the Lord was with Jesus to heal the sick.

Luke 5:17 NIV

The power of the Lord was present to heal them (plural), but very few experienced this power. This was due to unbelief.

Four devoted men carried a paralyzed man as far as they could go. There was no room in the house where Jesus taught, so their faith took them up. Faith always elevates! They began to do the unthinkable — they tore through a man's roof to get to Jesus. Unrestrained and unrestricted, their only concern was getting closer to Jesus. Anything that stands between you and Jesus should be destroyed. They presented the man to Jesus.

When Jesus saw their faith, he said, "Friend, your sins are forgiven."

LUKE 5:20 NIV

Salvation and healing go hand and hand. Simultaneous with Jesus forgiving his sins, the paralytic man is healed of his infirmity. Amazingly, the power of the Lord was present to heal "them." For the record, only one was healed.

A MAN'S SHADOW HEALS PEOPLE

Now that's a strange headline! A man's shadow heals people?

As a result, people brought the sick into the streets and laid them on beds and mats so that at least Peter's shadow might fall on some of them as he passed by. Crowds gathered also from the towns around Jerusalem, bringing their sick and those tormented by impure spirits, and all of them were healed.

ACTS 5:15-16 NIV

By definition, a shadow is a dark area that is produced because something has come between the light and the surface of a body. We have all lived in the dark. In the dark, we are subject to dark issues, dark problems. But Peter stands in the light. To stand in the light of God's presence is hope, health, and healing.

SLEEPING THROUGH MY BREAKTHROUGH

I had been complaining about my feet for weeks. The pain increased in intensity and frequency. Before long, I was experiencing continual discomfort when I walked. When I rested, they throbbed with agonizing pain.

Over the counter medicine was not working, so I finally broke down and made an appointment with a podiatrist. I was diagnosed with plantar fasciitis, often referred to as "policeman's heel." This was producing agonizing pain in both of my feet. I prayed constantly, but nothing seemed to be happening. In fact, it seemed to be getting worse.

The podiatrist said I needed to stay off my feet for an extended period of time, preferably a month. Who can stay off their feet for a month? Not me. He wanted to make casts for both feet, but I refused. That was nonnegotiable. I wasn't trying to be difficult, it just seemed so extreme. Instead, he gave me cortisone shots in both feet and recommended I do my best to stay off them. This temporarily blocked the pain, but after a few days, I was back in the same condition, suffering with chronic pain. For me, there seemed to be no cure.

> *"Healing is a matter of time, but it is sometimes also a matter of opportunity."*
>
> HIPPOCRATES, PRECEPTS

One Sunday afternoon, I was resting between our morning and evening services. I was undone; I had faked it so long, trying to give the appearance of wellness while suffering with excruciating pain. As I fell off to sleep, I was consciously aware of my aching feet.

I drifted off to sleep and experienced the most profound dream. The dream lasted for just a few seconds, but the result has been longstanding. This is what happened in my dream: A man in a brilliant white robe appeared before me. He was suspended over the galaxy, wearing a white robe with radiant,

> To stand in the light of God's presence is hope, health, and healing.

majestic colors. That's right - a white robe that radiated brilliant, glorious colors. With arms wide open, he spoke one word.

Meanwhile, I was watching myself stand before the spiritual being in my dream. I tried to mimic the word spoken. It was a linguistic impossibility; I could not articulate any part of the word.

Everything in a dream doesn't always make sense; this was one of those occurrences. I said to myself, "He said you're healed." I then replied to myself, "No, he said he has mended a relationship problem." I again responded to myself, saying, "No, he said he has fixed your finances." Why was I communicating within myself concerning these three areas?

Nothing God does or says is insignificant. Before that dream, I had three critical areas in my life that needed immediate attention, and I had exhausted all of my resources. The three concerns were my feet, my friends, and my finances.

The short dream was over and I awoke, wide-eyed. It was as if I were in the emergency room being hit with a defibrillator—clear!

Before the dream, rising to my feet had been a slow, laborious process but not now! In short order, I sprang from the bed. No pain whatsoever! Astonished at this inconceivable transaction, I felt like I was still dreaming, but I wasn't. I was totally cognizant and completely healed! Hallelujah!

As I was raising myself from the bed, a string of words proceeded from my mouth. This is what I said:

> *He sent his word, and healed them, and delivered them from their destructions.*
>
> Psalms 107:20 KJV

It didn't end there! Within 24 hours, I received a financial miracle, a bitter relational conflict was resolved (without any effort on my part), and I was physically healed.

When I talked back and forth to myself in the dream, I literally spoke into existence the three areas of my life the Holy Spirit would touch: my friends, my feet, and my finances. Now, that's amazing! My belief is that God always wants us to participate in our own deliverance, being totally aware that He alone receives the glory.

> *When I talked back and forth to myself in the dream, I literally spoke into existence the three areas of my life the Holy Spirit would touch.*

The Working of Miracles

The working of miracles is a supernatural gift that changes the natural order of things. Miracles operate in conjunction with faith.

In my early years of ministry, I was responsible for everything related to the church. One Saturday afternoon, I was using a push mower to cut the small churchyard. The mower would run momentarily, then shut off. I was cutting the grass ten yards at a time, first down after first down—I was so frustrated. Finally, the mower gave up; without two weeks' notice, it just quit. I pulled the chord again and again.

Around the same time, Agnes, one of our senior adults who lived nearby, was walking across the churchyard. She often walked by from her assisted living apartment to the grocery store. Agnes would laugh at this, but it was like watching paint dry. I'm not saying she was slow, but erosion is faster. Walking by with her girlish smile, she waved as she moved slowly on. (Picture a snail crawling through peanut butter.)

So she resumes her walk and I act busy. I'm waiting because I don't want her to see my disappointment and frustration with the mower. At this point, I have pulled the chord until my arm is sore. Then Agnes turned and came towards me. She asks, "What's wrong with your mower?"

"I think it's done," I say.

"Have you prayed?" she says.

"Uuuuuummm…," I mumble back.

She says, "Let's pray!"

We have a good prayer. She's a good lady, bless her heart. She means well. After all of these years, it's actually very sweet to see Agnes still conscious of the power of prayer. As her spiritual leader, I do my part to oblige her. But to Agnes, this is no perfunctory duty, it's entirely different. This is not a precious, tender moment. No, this is war.

Prayer is not a ritual but a relationship. I was about to be sent back to the second grade. Faith 101 is now in session.

Amen, she wraps it up — she's finally done. So I thank her, hug her, and say goodbye. She turns to walk towards her apartment, and I wait, and wait, and wait…

She turns back sternly and commands, "Pull the chord!" A bit embarrassed, I pull. Amazingly it cranks — I'm actually shocked! So I smile and wave, hoping for her to leave now (this year). I predict it will run for about ten yards then give up the ghost. So to protect her feelings, I meander about pretending to cut the grass. Unsatisfied with my productivity, she stops, turns around, and glares. Who is she to question my speed, molasses? She's so cantankerous. She won't leave — the nerve!

> When facing doubts I still hear Agnes' timeless words, "Pull the Chord...Now, Mow!"
>
> Faith without action is not faith at all.

Finally, I look at her. She challenges me and adamantly says, "Mow!" She is committed to the process and confident of the results. So I mow, cautiously pushing, expecting failure to ruin this "faith" moment. I push slowly, leaning into the mower until she's out of sight. "Whew!" Now back to real life, I go to work—and work, and work, and work... The little mower will not stop! Even the sound of it has a different frequency than before.

After I have cut the grass, I need a stick to pull the spark plug wire off, so that the mower will stop! It still wants to run. I would never have thought a little mower could bring so much conviction on someone. I then praised God while simultaneously asking for forgiveness.

When facing doubts I still hear Agnes' timeless words, "Pull the Chord...Now, Mow!" Faith without action is not faith at all.

GRACE PRODUCES WONDERMENT

The working of miracles is a gift from God to benefit others. This is a special grace that produces wonderment, as the impossible becomes possible through the obedience of the believer through whom the gift operates.

Miracles are a supernatural intervention of the Holy Spirit that bring profound change. Through miracles, the Holy Spirit offers solutions for our chaotic existence.

The apostle Paul's contemporaries understood the explosive power implied in his use of the phrase "working of miracles." The Greek word translated "miracles" is *dunamis*, the same root word we use in English for "dynamite." It's defined by *Strong's* as "physical power, force, might, ability, efficacy, energy, powerful deeds, deeds showing (physical) power." *HELPS Word Studies* definition includes "ability to perform; for the believer, power to achieve by applying the Lord's inherent abilities. Power through God's ability." *Dunamis* is the application of God's explosive, supernatural power on Earth.

The working of miracles and the gift of healings often collaborate. Miracles, faith, and healing often accompany one another. All of these channels work singly or in combination to exalt and extend the glory of God on Earth.

Miracles were a major part of the ministry of Jesus Christ as seen in healing blind eyes, lame men walking, multiplying fish and bread, or walking on water. These are just a few examples of the miraculous power of God. Signs and wonders follow those who believe.

Very truly I tell you, whoever believes in me will do the works I have been doing, and they will do even greater things than these, because I am going to the Father.

JOHN 14:12 NIV

GOD USES STUFF

Often it is an object or an act that serves to distinguish the working of miracles. Something natural may be implemented for the miraculous process to occur. Some examples of everyday objects used in the implementation of a miracle are clay for the blind man's eyes, a jawbone as Samson's weapon of arms, and a boy's small lunch for feeding the masses.

Natural objects such as Moses' rod or the widow's jug of oil were supernaturally used to ignite miraculous results. Understand that the

Supernatural Power on Earth

> The end result never testifies to the power of the thing used; rather, it testifies to a God that gets results out of anything!

object is nothing. It is merely a point of contact. It is not the focus, like a magic wand or lucky rabbit's foot — it's just not anything special or extraordinary of itself. The end result never testifies to the power of the thing used; rather, it testifies to a God that can get results out of anything! What a mighty God we serve! A God that can get results out of anything!

Of course, the Holy Spirit is not limited to the use of an action or an object; the miracle may occur "just because." The Spirit cannot be cornered or simply defined. The Spirit is like the wind, undefined and uncontrolled.

MIRACLES VALIDATE AND CONFIRM

Miracles always underscore the presence of God and validity of the truth and power of the gospel.

> *My message and my preaching were not with wise and persuasive words, but with a demonstration of the Spirit's power, so that your faith might not rest on human wisdom, but on God's power.*
>
> 1 CORINTHIANS 2:4-5 NIV

Miracles serve as a direct and dramatic demonstration of the presence of God's Spirit. And the presence brings us comfort in knowing that we are close to the person. The same Hebrew word *paneh* is translated as "presence" and also as "face." (See Exodus 33:14 and 2 Chronicles 7:14 where the same word is used interchangeably.) The Spirit comes in power to heighten our awareness of the presence of

God, affirming that His face is turned toward us in love and miraculous supply of every kind.

INGRID'S STORY

Years ago, our church started doing short-term missions in the remote, impoverished areas between the Dominican Republic and Haitian border. We have always seen God move there. I attribute the miraculous success to limited options. In America, we can visit a doctor any time of day or night. However, in the mountainous and rugged terrain of the Dominican, it's not always that easy. I've found that miracles occur when options are limited and you need them most. Miracles are necessary when there is no other recourse.

> *Miracles always underscore the validity of the truth and power of the gospel. They serve as a direct and dramatic demonstration of the presence of God's Spirit.*

Ingrid is a faithful minister in San Cristobal, Dominican Republic. She is a courageous, small-statured, hard-working mother and minister. Ingrid has been a committed Christian and beautiful example of the love of Christ from the first time I met her. Her walk with God has been unwavering — she truly loves the Lord.

When I first met her, she had the reputation of taking her small income to cover the nakedness of little girls. Before I ever heard her minister, I saw her minister. Her passion and burden of love was to put underwear on the small girls in the village, many of which had been sexually abused and accustomed to walking without undergarments.

As the years passed by, I watched her children grow to be incredible servants of the Lord, following in their precious mother's footsteps. She has always been a faithful wife and consecrated minister to the

Supernatural Power on Earth

community. Unfortunately, Ingrid's husband did not share the same spiritual values. Like many men in that area, he lived by different standards. I believe he has loved his family, but a double-minded man is unstable to say the least.

Ingrid's husband worked for the army, so his position was respected in the village. With his prestigious position, he didn't have much use for the things of God, which Ingrid considered most important. This was hard on the marriage and difficult for the children to witness. But she pressed on.

He was unfaithful and violent, his raging temper fueled when he became inebriated. When he drank alcohol, as he often did, things would quickly get out of hand.

On a particular weekend of drinking and arguing, things rapidly went awry. Our team had just left two days prior to this incident, so we were in constant communication with the pastors of San Cristobal and their village community. When the devastating news got back to us, we were deeply saddened.

Ingrid had been shot in the chest with a 45, her husband's gun. The bullet had entered through her left side, just above the heart, and the exit wound was straight out of her back. Everyone on our team was shocked. She had just fed us meals, washed our dishes, ministered with us in the churches. She had even made us gifts. How could this happen to Ingrid? We were baffled.

We were told that her husband had been drinking and had become very angry. In his belligerent state, he wielded his army-issued revolver. The aftermath of this careless act was Ingrid lying on the floor with a hole in her chest and her children traumatized.

The community responded immediately. It is extremely uncommon to even hear gunfire in the small village community. She was rushed to the closest medical center possible. Her church family at home and abroad began to pray fervently. She had lost a lot of blood and prompt treatment was far from available.

This incident happened on a Friday. Three days later on a Monday afternoon, Ingrid walked out of the hospital without assistance. She had stitches in the front of her chest and on her back. Every vital organ and every major artery had been miraculously avoided. The straight-line trajectory of the 45 bullet went in and out, undisturbed by bone or critical mass. She was a walking miracle!

A few months later, my wife and I were able to personally examine the entry and exit wounds that Ingrid now carries. Her healing scars were more than a conversation piece; they were the evidence of the supernatural power of God on Earth. Her body was now a visible canvas, bearing the marks of the Spirit's intervention.

THE POWER GIFTS DEMONSTRATE THE NATURE OF GOD

The working of miracles can occur because of concentrated prayer, uncompromised faith, or simply as an act of God's sovereignty. Miracles override natural laws and predictable outcomes. Miracles are a sign for the believer and the unbeliever. As everyone, and I mean everyone, prayed for a miracle for Ingrid, God began to move through the Holy Spirit. The manifestation of a miracle is to benefit us all — the good, the bad, and the ugly. Miracles are indicative of God's character, not the approval of ours. Miracles bring glory to God.

> *Miracles are indicative of God's character, not the approval of ours. Miracles bring glory to God.*

The power gifts are dramatic demonstrations of the nature and presence of God. They contradict the natural reality and delve into the supernatural dimension. They provide the supernatural *dunamis* power to help you do what needs to be done.

The manifestation of these gifts can be observed immediately or progressively; either way, they are life-altering. They can produce something out of nothing. They demonstrate God's care and provision right here on Earth. Ultimately, they build the Kingdom while bringing attention to Jesus and confirming His Word.

Chapter 9

POWER ON
TONGUES, INTERPRETATION, & PROPHECY

All nine of the spiritual gifts are from the same Holy Spirit, each reflecting an aspect of God's nature. The apostle Paul made sure the Corinthian church understood this because in their culture the oracles represented multiple gods. Our God imparts various gifts to His people through one and the same Spirit.

> *There are different kinds of gifts, but the same Spirit distributes them. There are different kinds of service, but the same Lord. There are different kinds of working, but in all of them and in everyone it is the same God at work.... To one there is given through the Spirit ...prophecy...to another speaking in different kinds of tongues, and to still another the interpretation of tongues. All these are the work of one and the same Spirit, and he distributes them to each one, just as he determines.*
>
> 1 CORINTHIANS 12:4-11 NIV

Vocal gifts may be the least understood of all. A lot of fear, false teaching, and false teachers have surrounded these controversial gifts.

The controversy concerning vocal gifts is nothing more than a satanic strategy to prevent you from receiving, using, and benefitting from these powerful gifts. Satan would rather you disengage from these particular gifts than for him to suffer the consequences of you possessing them. Understanding this concept will help you to see that this matter will never be "cleared up," because Satan will always be threatened by these gifts in operation. Because of this threat, Satan will always cast doubt and confusion where the vocal gifts are concerned.

> Your voice is so powerful; Satan will stop at nothing to keep you silent.

Your voice is so powerful Satan will stop at nothing to keep you silent. This is why we constructively study God's Word for ultimate truth. God's Word gives us enough boldness to stand and enough brokenness to stand again when we have stumbled.

I urge you to open your mind to discussion and, more importantly, to open your heart to the Spirit's voice. Do not allow bias to bind you. The Holy Spirit has promised to be a Teacher — all He needs is a student.

The first words that God spoke to Abraham were "leave home!" Everyone who wants a personal relationship with the Holy Spirit must eventually "leave home." Home is the safe and familiar, but the promise of God's Spirit is so much more gratifying than anything you could experience "at home."

THE CASE FOR CONTINUATIONISM

Cessationism is the belief that the gifts of the Holy Spirit, especially tongues, supernatural signs, and prophecy, have ceased for today. Continuationism is the belief that the gifts of the Spirit have never ceased to be in operation and continue to function in the church today. According to the false theory of cessationism, the New Testament church should no longer encourage or attempt to operate in these giftings. Many cessationists have become outspoken, even to the degree of saying that the baptism of the Holy Ghost is "of the Devil." This is a dangerous area to critique because blaspheming the Holy Spirit is the only unpardonable sin. (Read more on this topic in Chaper 10.) Therefore, we must take extreme caution when broadcasting opinion as doctrine. This is a slippery slope.

If you were raised or influenced by a cessationist, you've probably allowed the prevailing thought to override any spiritual promptings or interest on your part. Many just leave theology to the theologian, while the Bible says to work out your own salvation. Just because someone has a degree in an area does not mean that they fully know and understand what they have studied. This happens in every field of study and is why that even in professional fields there is abuse through ignorance.

To know God's voice is to hear God's voice. If outside voices are louder than the internal voice of God's Spirit, it is time to retrain your ears.

So then faith comes by hearing, and hearing by the word of God.

ROMANS 10:17 NKJV

A fair biblical perspective is found when searching all of the scriptures concerning the Holy Spirit and the gifts He distributes and by applying the scriptures as seen in context.

There are many strong reasons to know the gifts of the Spirit continue in our day and many excellent resources making the case for continuationism. A key verse in which the point is clearly made is found in Paul's first epistle to the Corinthians:

I always thank my God for you because of his grace given you in Christ Jesus. For in him you have been enriched in every way—with all kinds of speech and with all knowledge—...Therefore you do not lack any spiritual gift as you eagerly wait for our Lord Jesus Christ to be revealed.

1 Corinthians 1:4-7 NIV

According to this passage, if Jesus has not returned, every gift should be available and operational. For the record, Jesus has not returned! My recommendation for you is to receive while waiting for His return!

In addition to this verse, Paul speaks further to the Corinthians on this topic. Some have used this passage to say that prophecy and tongues have ceased. But careful reading will cause one to admit that knowledge hasn't passed away, therefore these vocal gifts haven't either. In fact, rather than passing away, the prophet Daniel foretold that knowledge will *increase* in the latter days.

But where there are prophecies, they will cease; where there are tongues, they will be stilled; where there is knowledge, it will pass away. For we know in part and we prophesy in part, but when completeness comes, what is in part disappears...For now we see only a reflection as in a mirror; then we shall see face to face. Now I know in part; then I shall know fully, even as I am fully known.

1 Corinthians 13:8-12 NIV

At this time in history, we still have only partial knowedge and can see only as a reflection. When Christ returns for His people, we will fully know, even as we are fully known. So we can be assured that the Spirit's gifts are still in operation, understanding that the fullness of times and of knowledge have yet to be fulfilled. We also have the witness of the church fathers, as well as medically verified proof of miracles happening today. We can be confident in His Word and the power of His Spirit at work in us, just as He promised!

THREE VOCAL GIFTS

There are three vocal gifts, sometimes also referred to as utterance gifts. These are tongues, interpretation, and prophecy.

THE GIFT OF TONGUES

> *When the day of Pentecost came, they were all together in one place. Suddenly a sound like the blowing of a violent wind came from heaven and filled the whole house where they were sitting. They saw what seemed to be tongues of fire that separated and came to rest on each of them. All of them were filled with the Holy Spirit and began to speak in other tongues as the Spirit enabled them.*
>
> ACTS 2:2-4 NIV

The gift of tongues is powerful evidence of the Holy Spirit's impartation. This is without doubt the most controversial of all nine gifts. The gift of tongues is a supernatural utterance of a heavenly or earthly language. The gift of tongues is also known as the gift of languages. It may be used in a prayer language to God or as a witness for God.

This is a gift, so it is not learned or earned. This gift is available to all believers, not just a select few.

Manifestation of Baptism in the Holy Spirit

In the chronicles of the early church's growth found in the book of Acts, the gift of tongues is seen as evidence of baptism in the Holy Spirit. While not specifically stated in every account, it can be deduced that all did receive this gift at some point in their experience as a believer. Read and consider the following accounts:

1. The one hundred and twenty believers praying in the upper room. "All of them were filled with the Holy Spirit and began to speak in other tongues as the Spirit enabled them" (Acts 2:4).

2. The Samaritans (Acts 8:14-17). Here it's clearly stated that the baptism the apostles were sent to impart was not the same event as, and subsequent to, water baptism. When the sorcerer Simon saw the Holy Ghost was given by the laying on of the apostles' hands, he wanted to buy the power to do the same thing. It's evident there was a physical manifestation; it's likely he saw and heard the Samaritans speak in tongues.

3. Paul's experience (Acts 9:10-19). In this account, it's not stated that Paul spoke with tongues when he was baptized in the Holy Spirit. However, he later wrote, "I thank God that I speak in tongues more than all of you" (1 Corinthians 14:18). If we assume the pattern is consistent, he likely began to speak with tongues when he was baptized in the Spirit.

4. Cornelius and his household (Acts 10:44-48). The Jewish "believers who had come with Peter were astonished that the gift of the Holy Spirit had been poured out even on Gentiles. For they heard them speaking in tongues and praising God."

5. The Ephesians (Acts 19:1-6). "When they heard this, they were baptized in the name of the Lord Jesus. And when Paul had laid

his hands upon them, the Holy Spirit came on them, and they began speaking with tongues and prophesying."

Some have suggested that speaking in tongues is merely emotionalism. Emotions come from the soulish realm. The soul is eternal and immortal, consisting of your mind, will, and emotions. Therefore, emotions, like the soul, are eternal. You cannot discount speaking in tongues as merely emotionalism or fanaticism because if we say, "It's just emotions," we must also say, "It's more than emotional, it's eternal."

In worship to God, I commit my mind, body, soul, and spirit. I like to feel the Spirit! I need to feel the spirit! In fact, the fruit of the Spirit consists of powerful qualities that can be felt on an emotional level, such as love, joy, peace, etc. God has given us feelings, so I will use what He has given me. If you can have it and not feel it, you can lose it and not know it. Ask the Holy Spirit for tangible experiences that can be felt.

Why the Tongue?

Like you, I have had my share of opposition. I've even encountered enemies along the way. But to date, the greatest difficulties I have experienced have been a result of my own tongue! After all, the power of life and death are in my own tongue. I have been hung by the tongue more times than I'd like to admit.

But no human being can tame the tongue. It is a restless evil, full of deadly poison.

James 3:8 NIV

According to this passage, no man can tame the tongue. It is unruly and out of control. Yielding yourself completely to God's Spirit allows even the conflict-creating tongue to be controlled by God.

Look at the ships also, though they are so great and are driven by strong winds, are still directed by a very small rudder wherever the inclination of the pilot desires. So also the tongue is a small part of the body, and yet it boasts of great things.

See how great a forest is set aflame by such a small fire! And the tongue is a fire, the very world of iniquity; the tongue is set among our members as that which defiles the entire body, and sets on fire the course of our life, and is set on fire by hell.

JAMES 3:4-6 NIV

> The tongue is the rudder of your life.

A small tongue can create big problems. We have witnessed the devastation of wildfire raging out of control, all because of a single careless match. James warns us of the tragic aftermath our tongue can produce.

The tongue is the rudder of your life; it directs where you go. Whether in compliance or not, your tongue is steering your ship.

Brothers and sisters, stop thinking like children. In regard to evil be infants, but in your thinking be adults. In the Law it is written:

"With other tongues and through the lips of foreigners I will speak to this people, but even then they will not listen to me, says the Lord."

1 CORINTHIANS 14:20-21 NIV

Through the Holy Spirit, God redeems our tongue. He uses that same unruly member to bring glory to His name.

Careless words, anger and hostility, unguarded moments—these have brought out the worst in us. We say in regret, "I wish I could take that back."

The Holy Spirit redeems our tongue. The Spirit brings course correction. In short, we are taking it back. This is counterintuitive, but through the surrender of our tongue, we regain authority and control.

The Tongue as a Sign

Tongues, then, are a sign, not for believers but for unbelievers...

1 Corinthians 14:22 NIV

This phenomenon in which a person speaks in a language unknown to them is called *xenolalia*. The words are spoken in an understandable language, such as Russian or French, but is one unknown to the speaker. To my knowledge, I have not experienced this myself, but I do know many who have. One in particular could carry on a natural conversation in a foreign language.

This is what happened on the Day of Pentecost when the Spirit was first poured out on the church. There were people from many nations speaking many languages, who had come to Jerusalem for the Feast of Pentecost (or Firstfruits). When the newly Spirit-baptized believers began to speak in tongues, other nationalities could hear the Holy Spirit speaking to them in their own languages.

Now there were staying in Jerusalem God-fearing Jews from every nation under heaven. And when this sound occurred, the

Supernatural Power on Earth

multitude came together, and were confused, because everyone heard them speak in his own language. Then they were all amazed and marveled, saying to one another, "Look, are not all these who speak Galileans? And how is it that we hear, each in our own language in which we were born? Parthians and Medes and Elamites, those dwelling in Mesopotamia, Judea and Cappadocia, Pontus and Asia, Phrygia and Pamphylia, Egypt and the parts of Libya adjoining Cyrene, visitors from Rome, both Jews and proselytes, Cretans and Arabs—we hear them speaking in our own tongues the wonderful works of God."

ACTS 2:5-11 NKJV

People from around the world had converged in Jerusalem for this time of feasting. One hundred twenty unlearned people tapped in to the Holy Spirit's power and began to vocally broadcast the message of God's glory in every language that was represented in Jerusalem. Astounded and amazed, over 3000 converts were added to the church by the end of the day.

> On the day of Pentecost, tongues as a sign became the door of utterance to reach beyond natural boundaries and limitations. This gift of the Spirit would enable the early disciples to evangelize the world.

Xenolalia was the entryway of communication to diverse people groups. Through the impact of this one day, the gospel would spread throughout the whole world. What began as addition turned in to multiplication. On the day of Pentecost, tongues as a sign became the door of utterance to reach beyond natural boundaries and limitations. This gift of the Spirit would enable the early disciples to evangelize the world.

Power On Tongues, Interpretation, & Prophecy

And pray for us, too, that God may open a door for our message, so that we may proclaim the mystery of Christ...

Colossians 4:3 NIV

Tongues as a Prayer Language

Tongues encourage, build, and strengthen the individual believer and the body as a whole.

But you, beloved, building yourselves up on your most holy faith, praying in the Holy Spirit.

Jude 20 NKJV

Anyone who speaks in a tongue edifies themselves...

1 Corinthians 14:4a NIV

Through the gift of tongues, the Holy Spirit has the unique ability to pray through a believer and make intercession unto God. This prayer is typically spoken to God in a language unknown to the one who is speaking. The Holy Spirit (the Spirit of truth) prays the right prayer to God.

As our natural prayers are often misinformed, we may inadvertently pray amiss. But when the Spirit prays through us, it is always according to the will of God. Paul touched on this aspect of Spirit-inspired prayer in the two passages below:

We know that the whole creation has been groaning as in the pains of childbirth right up to the present time. Not only so,

but we ourselves, who have the firstfruits of the Spirit, groan inwardly as we wait eagerly for our adoption to sonship... In the same way, the Spirit helps us in our weakness. We do not know what we ought to pray for, but the Spirit himself intercedes for us through wordless groans. And he who searches our hearts knows the mind of the Spirit, because the Spirit intercedes for God's people in accordance with the will of God.

ROMANS 8:22-27 NIV

For he who speaks in a tongue does not speak to men but to God, for no one understands him; however, in the spirit he speaks mysteries.

1 CORINTHIANS 14:2 NKJV

According to this passage, there are tongues that no man understands. In 1 Corinthians 13:1, Paul also made mention of speaking "in the tongues of angels," clearly not a language naturally known to human beings. Tongues as a private prayer language may not always be understood by the speaker or any other person. This language is not spoken unto man but unto God. This phenomenon is called *glossolalia*. As Paul explained, it's a devotional language that draws us closer to God. This prayer language enables us to go to a deeper level with God than human consciousness will allow.

However, as it is written: "What no eye has seen, what no ear has heard, and what no human mind has conceived" — the things God has prepared for those who love him—these are the things God has revealed to us by his Spirit.

> *The Spirit searches all things, even the deep things of God. For who knows a person's thoughts except their own spirit within them? In the same way no one knows the thoughts of God except the Spirit of God. What we have received is not the spirit of the world, but the Spirit who is from God, so that we may understand what God has freely given us. This is what we speak, not in words taught us by human wisdom but in words taught by the Spirit, explaining spiritual realities with Spirit-taught words.*
>
> 1 CORINTHIANS 2:9-13 NIV

This is not for human communication; this interaction is for God alone. When praying in tongues, the Spirit reclaims and redirects our prayer life. Our desires become aligned with God's will. We are then able to abort our selfish motives and ambition and relate to God through the Holy Spirit. This goes beyond His presence—we relate to His person. This is a special, supernatural, uninterrupted channel that speaks directly to God via Holy Spirit.

So you may ask, "Don't I always speak directly to God?" The answer is "yes and no." Yes, because God hears us, helps us, and loves us. No, because we never venture far from personal bias, experience, misinformation, and satanic interference.

How many times have you begun to pray while finding yourself mentally drifting into other thoughts and concerns? I'll answer for you—"Often!"

When we pray in this prayer language, we pray the prayer that works. When the Holy Spirit intercedes through us, we hit the mark every time. Even if we are unaware of what has been said,

> *When the Holy Spirit intercedes through us, something powerful has transpired in a completely different realm.*

something powerful has transpired in a completely different realm. Like the wind that we cannot see, its effects are undeniable.

... [I]mportunate prayer does not spring from physical vehemence or fleshly energy. It is not an impulse of energy, nor a mere earnestness of soul. It is a wrought force, a faculty implanted and aroused by the Holy Spirit. Virtually, it is the intercession of the Holy Spirit in us.

E.M. BOUNDS, *THE NECESSITY OF PRAYER*,
"PRAYER AND IMPORTUNITY"

In our natural language, we cannot even begin to express the depths of our heart. We lack the vocabulary to speak on this level. For instance, I love my wife, my dog, my truck. To use the same vocabulary in each instance can in no way be a true expression or representation of my deep love for my wife. Neither can human language do justice for the depth of love I have for the Triune God. There must be more! This is where the Holy Spirit intervenes. The Spirit prays through me and beyond me. This is not a linguistic exercise; this is beautiful, profound communication in the presence of the eternal God.

SETTING ORDER

The apostle Paul outlines proper protocol for use of this special prayer language. It is not to be disruptive in a corporate setting but to be utilized privately for the benefit of the one speaking to God.

This language can be used in public but not publicly. Let me explain: You can sing along with a choir even if you're not in the choir. As long as you are not drawing attention away from the designated worship leaders, you may sing without causing disruption to the service. The same is true in many corporate prayer settings: You can pray aloud but not too loudly so as not to be a distraction. This prayer language should never distract from the dynamic set for the corporate setting. Therefore, your payer language can be used in a gathering but never to overshadow or interrupt the common goal of corporate worship and edification.

The Gift of Interpretation of Tongues

Interpretation is the counterpart to the gift of tongues. Through this supernatural gift, the message spoken in an unknown language is made known or explained. This is an unlearned, supernatural ability to interpret the utterance with no prior understanding of the language in which the message was given. Through the gift of interpretation, the mystery is revealed.

> *For this reason, the one who speaks in a tongue should pray that they may interpret what they say. For if I pray in a tongue, my spirit prays, but my mind is unfruitful. So what shall I do? I will pray with my spirit, but I will also pray with my understanding; I will sing with my spirit, but I will also sing with my understanding.....What then shall we say, brothers and sisters? When you come together, each of you has a hymn, or a word of instruction, a revelation, a tongue or an interpretation. Everything must be done so that the church may be built up.*
>
> 1 Corinthians 14:13-15, 26

Interpretation gives human understanding to what the Spirit is saying. This is usually not a word for word translation; it's *the essence* of what God is saying through the Spirit. Interpretation means "to unfold the meaning of what is said, explain, expound." In the context and biblical sense, interpretation does not mean "translation."

For example, three truthful witnesses may see the same car accident. Though they use different words to explain what they saw, they are describing the same incident or truth. Similarly, with the gift of interpretation, the person operating in this gift allows the hearers to know what the mind of God is. He is relating the essence of what has been revealed, although this may not be a word for word, literal translation. (There have been cases where literal translations of a tongue were given following the Spirit's message in a foreign language. Whether speaking the essence of the message or the literal translation, God can achieve His ends through diverse means, as long as He has obedient people.)

Two things happen when this gift is in operation:

- The church or spiritual community is edified.
- God is glorified.

I would like every one of you to speak in tongues, but I would rather have you prophesy. The one who prophesies is greater than the one who speaks in tongues, unless someone interprets, so that the church may be edified.... So it is with you. Since you are eager for gifts of the Spirit, try to excel in those that build up the church. For this reason the one who speaks in a tongue should pray that they may interpret what they say.

1 CORINTHIANS 14:5-6, 12-13 NIV

The apostle Paul asserts that if a person prays in an unknown tongue, he should also pray to interpret. However, this is not restrictive so as to exclude any other participant from giving the interpretation, if it is within God's sovereign will.

Keep in mind, Paul encourages us to pray for the interpretation.

This prayer could even begin now, if you so desire to be used in this gift. The only prayer God can't answer is the prayer you don't pray.

Therefore, my brothers and sisters, be eager to prophesy, and do not forbid speaking in tongues. But everything should be done in a fitting and orderly way.

1 Corinthians 14:39-40 NIV

As with the gift of prophecy, an interpretation of tongues should be judged or weighed to discern that it is consistent with God's nature and character, as well as Scripture. Holy Spirit-inspired words will never contradict His word, character, will, or purposes. Spiritual utterances do not create confusion or fear; rather, they promote peace and clarity.

THE GIFT OF PROPHECY

For you can all prophesy in turn so that everyone may be instructed and encouraged. The spirits of prophets are subject to the control of prophets. For God is not a God of disorder but of peace—as in all the congregations of the Lord's people.

1 Corinthians 14:31-33 NIV

The book of Numbers records a time when the Lord poured the spirit of prophecy upon the elders of Israel. Perhaps in an attempt to preserve Moses' role as leader and prophet to the people, Joshua felt they should be forbidden from prophesying. In response to Joshua's request that Moses restrain them from doing so, he expressed the desire that all God's people would prophesy.

> *But Moses replied, "Are you jealous for my sake? I wish that all the LORD's people were prophets and that the LORD would put his Spirit on them!"*
>
> NUMBERS 11:29 NIV

Through the baptism and gifts of the Spirit, Moses' prayer was answered! Paul confirms this when he wrote, "I would like *every one of you* to speak in tongues, but I would rather have you prophesy.... When you come together, *each of you* has a hymn, or a word of instruction, a revelation, a tongue or an interpretation.... For *you can all prophesy* in turn so that everyone may be instructed and encouraged" (1 Cor. 14:5, 26, 31 *emphasis added*).

Prophecy is a gift to the whole body which reveals God's will to the people. God's intentions become clear and uncertainty loses its fearful grip. Through prophetic words, we are given supernatural revelation and insight into the mind of God.

PROPHECY IS THE PREFERRED GIFT

> *Prophecy is the preferred gift and singularly called out as the one to be eagerly desired.*

Prophecy is the highest order of all the gifts. Prophecy is considered priority. We should earnestly strive for all the gifts, but prophecy is most useful in that it brings direction and clarity to the body. Therefore, prophecy is the preferred gift.

Isaiah tells us that Gods ways and thoughts are higher than ours, and His ways are past finding out. Prophecy is the antidote to this dilemma and is the gift singularly called out for us to eagerly desire. See the following translations of 1 Corinthians 14:1, which indicate how we should pursue this gift above all others.

Pursue love and desire spiritual gifts, but especially that you may prophesy. (NKJV)

Follow the way of love and eagerly desire gifts of the Spirit, especially prophecy. (NIV)

Let love be your highest goal! But you should also desire the special abilities the Spirit gives--especially the ability to prophesy. (NLT)

Be eager in your pursuit of this Love, and be earnestly ambitious for spiritual gifts, but let it be chiefly so in order that you may prophesy. (WNT)

Eagerly pursue and seek to acquire [this] love [make it your aim, your great quest]; and earnestly desire and cultivate the spiritual endowments (gifts), especially that you may prophesy (interpret the divine will and purpose in inspired preaching and teaching). (AMPC)

In 1 Corinthians 14:3, Paul states the purpose of prophecy: "But the one who prophesies speaks to people for their strengthening, encouraging and comfort." In the King James version, it reads as "edification, and exhortation, and comfort." It is useful in the recognition of compromise, as well as building up and giving comfort to those suffering, persecuted, or discouraged. When the Lord speaks to His people through this gift, they are given strength to keep pressing on, find joy and spiritual enrichment, and are lifted to new heights in worship and service.

Even if correction is spoken, divinely inspired prophecy edifies. Edification means to build up, not tear down. Prophecy may expose wrong motives and wrong intentions, but even then it brings peace, comfort, and restoration.

Judging Prophecy

Prophecy can be mishandled or abused. When this happens, prophetic words may be meanspirited or judgmental. Like dynamite, words can be used for construction or destruction. This is why it is imperative for prophecy, as well as the equivalent tongues and interpretation, to be judged. Prophecy must be exposed to scrutiny; if it can't be tested, it can't be trusted.

Two or three prophets should speak, and the others should weigh carefully what is said.

1 Corinthians 14:29 NIV

The Greek word *diakrino* is here translated in the *New International Version* as "weigh carefully." The *King James Version* of the Bible translates it as "judge." *Strong's* definition is "to separate, distinguish, discern one thing from another"; *Thayers'*, "to separate, make a distinction, discriminate"; *HELPS Word Studies*, "to investigate (judge) thoroughly – literally, judging 'back-and-forth' which can either (positively) refer to close-reasoning (descrimination) or negatively 'over-judging' (going too far, vacillating)."

We shouldn't blindly accept anything spoken by another; neither should we be suspicious and critical, entirely rejecting a prophetic word by "negatively over-judging." In other words, we take the time to listen and weigh, separate by making a distinction, then hold on to the good. We simply reject that which may be tainted by the speaker's personal bias or mental filters.

In natural terms, as pure water flows through a pipe it sometimes picks up bits of rust or dirt along the way. While the water is beneficial and should be retained, the impurities should be discarded. To use another everyday example, when you eat a piece of chicken or fish, you separate the beneficial from the unpalatable; you chew and digest the meat, discarding the bones, gristle, or scales.

Do not quench the Spirit. Do not treat prophecies with contempt but test them all; hold on to what is good, reject every kind of evil.

1 Thessalonians 5:19-22 NIV

The Holy Spirit lives inside every believer, giving us the ability to discern good from evil and truth from deception. When impure prophetic words are spoken from a motive of pride, greed, or manipulation, something within you is grieved. It doesn't ring true. When God truly speaks through another believer, your heart and spirit rejoice in the truth.

The apostles John and Peter provide additional instruction in the following passages:

I am writing these things to you about those who are trying to lead you astray. As for you, the anointing you received from him remains in you, and you do not need anyone to teach you. But as his anointing teaches you about all things and as that anointing is real, not counterfeit—just as it has taught you, remain in him.

1 John 2:26-27 NIV

Dear friends, do not believe every spirit, but test the spirits to see whether they are from God, because many false prophets have gone out into the world. This is how you can recognize the Spirit of God: Every spirit that acknowledges that Jesus Christ has come in the flesh is from God, but every spirit that does not acknowledge Jesus is not from God. This is the spirit of the antichrist, which you have heard is coming and even now is already in the world. You, dear children, are from God and have overcome them, because the one who is in you is greater than the one who is in the world. They are from the world and therefore speak from the viewpoint of the world, and the world listens to them. We are from God, and whoever knows God listens to us; but whoever is not from God does not listen to us. This is how we recognize the Spirit of truth and the spirit of falsehood.

1 John 4:1-4 NIV

But there were also false prophets among the people, just as there will be false teachers among you. They will secretly introduce destructive heresies, even denying the sovereign Lord who bought them—bringing swift destruction on themselves. Many will follow their depraved conduct and will bring the way of truth into disrepute. In their greed these teachers will exploit you with fabricated stories. Their condemnation has long been hanging over them, and their destruction has not been sleeping.

2 Peter 2:1-3 NIV

Do not allow spiritual vetting to discourage you from being used in the gift of prophecy. It should actually make you feel safe. Anything of value attracts thieves, and everything of value should be heavily guarded. Restated, if you do not guard things of value, you have failed to place value in what should be protected.

Prophecy a Creative, Redemptive Power

At its highest level, prophecy is creative. We see this in the creation narrative, "And God said let there be... and there was...." When the Lord speaks through the gift of prophecy, or tongues and interpretation, creative power is released to bring His will and purposes to pass in the lives of individuals, the church, or a region.

> *Prophetic words, as well as tongues and interpretation, release creative power to bring God's purposes to pass in the lives of individuals, the church, or a region.*

Prophecy is not bound by time. This gift may be used in foretelling futuristic events or for exposing present circumstances. It may also be used to establish context and credibility by revealing past events. It may be preaching the word, explaining previous prophecies, or making future prophetic declarations. In the last days, prophecy is to be used to reach the world. God desires this gift for all believers.

> *[I]f an unbeliever or an inquirer comes in while everyone is prophesying, they are convicted of sin and are brought under judgment by all, as the secrets of their hearts are laid bare. So they will fall down and worship God, exclaiming, "God is really among you!"*
>
> 1 Corinthians 14:24-25 NIV

> *In the last days, God says, I will pour out my Spirit on all people. Your sons and daughters will prophesy, your young men will see visions, your old men will dream dreams.*
>
> Acts 2:17 NIV

Personal Prophecy

I am thankful because God has surrounded my life with prophetic voices. These are prophets though they may never hang that shingle above their door. And these are not self-proclaimed prophets; they are just Spirit-led people who hear from God and speak His message. (It's more important to function in the gift than to require you be called by a title.) If you truly desire direction, God will place watchmen around you like guardrails through treacherous mountain roads; they will help you avoid danger.

A person finds joy in giving an apt reply—and how good is a timely word!

PROVERBS 15:23 NIV

My Grandmother Carrie always called me out (prophesied) to be a preacher. I never got used to that. It made me very uncomfortable. She would place her hand on my tiny shoulder and say, "You will minister to thousands!" Under my breath I would say, "Not me!"

In high school, out of hundreds of students, I was voted the shyest by my peers. What an awesome superlative, right? Though I was actively involved in sports and had many friends, I was awkward and timid. Introverted and self-conscious—who wouldn't want that skill set? In my senior yearbook I was forced to pose for a picture behind a door with just my eyes and forehead looking out. How embarrassing! Not most athletic or best looking; no, the shyest! I felt like a prairie dog, and I just wanted to be left alone.

I performed well as a student, but can you guess what class I almost failed in college? Public speaking. I can remember being emotionally terrified as I read 5 minute speeches in front of 25 people. It seemed like the whole world was watching me as I wiped sweat from my brow and my lips quivered. This class was torture—nausea, diarrhea, the sweats; this was no laughing matter. Called to preach? Sure, Grandma, whatever you say.

But at 27 years old, after my grandmother had died, I took up the mantle God had intended for me to wear all the while. God chooses whom man rejects; man often rejects whom God will choose. Called to preach? Absolutely! Multiple times a week I stand and deliver a message without side effects, thank God!

This is proof once again that your condition is not your conclusion. When God decides something, all of the power behind those words are activated into fulfilling His purpose.

The LORD Almighty has sworn, "Surely, as I have planned, so it will be, and as I have purposed, so it will happen.

ISAIAH 14:24 NIV

Then said the Lord to me, You have seen well, for I am alert and active, watching over My word to perform it.

JEREMIAH 1:12 AMPC

FALSE PROPHECY

Thus says the Lord GOD, "Woe to the foolish prophets who are following their own spirit and have seen nothing. O Israel, your prophets have been like foxes among ruins."

EZEKIEL 13:3-4 NIV

Unfortunately, the body of Christ has been plagued with charlatans who self-promote and manipulate people for selfish gain. In the Sermon on the Mount, Jesus warned His followers saying, "Watch out for false prophets. They come to you in sheep's clothing, but inwardly they are ferocious wolves."

The counterfeit gifts often cast doubt and confusion over the gifts of God. Through deception, people become disillusioned. Counterfeit money only proves that there is authentic currency of real worth. So anything of intrinsic value will always have a copy.

How do I know what's true and what's false? In the banking industry, employees are trained to identify counterfeit bills by studying real currency, not the reverse. When you are familiar with the legitimate, you will immediately recognize the counterfeit. So it is with spiritual fakes—when you are intimate with the Spirit and the truth of the Word, you will recognise the false when it presents itself.

False prophets can be identified by their "fruit." After His warning about the wolves, Jesus said, "By their fruit you will recognize them. Do people pick grapes from thornbushes, or figs from thistles? Likewise, every good tree bears good fruit, but a bad tree bears bad fruit. A good tree cannot bear bad fruit, and a bad tree cannot bear good fruit."

Examine the fruit by asking if they bear the fruit of the Spirit, reflecting His nature. (See Galatians 5:22-23; Ephesians 5:9-10; Colossians 3:12.) Do they have something to personally gain? Motivations help to reveal the origin of a word. Also examine what is the result, or fruit and outward manifestation, of their teachings. Is the flock being financially drained? Are they sexually promiscuous or adulterous, or do they hold biblical moral values? Do they believe they are the only group who are "right," separating themselvs from other godly ministers and influences? Or do they show love and unity with the body of Christ?

These characteristics and more identify false teachers who devour people's lives. Their final end was foretold by Jesus in the above passage: "Every tree that does not bear good fruit is cut down and thrown into the fire."

Not every "prophetic" word is strictly Spirit-inspired or of demonic origin. Someone may have good intentions and speak presumptuously; this does not make them a false prophet. This may not be satanic, just not very smart. This is why we test the "prophetic" word. Even if it comes from someone you trust, the word must stand trial. This is not to belittle or undermine another; rather, to stay within the guardrails so that you don't run off the way that leads to life.

A SEER'S PERSPECTIVE

"Listen to me, Judah and people of Jerusalem! Have faith in the LORD your God and you will be upheld; have faith in his prophets and you will be successful."

2 CHRONICLES 20:20B NIV

In the Old Testament, some prophets were known as seers. (See 1 Samuel 9:9.) We call perfect vision 20/20. In 2 Chronicles 20:20 quoted above, God instructs us to believe the seer. A prophetic word can easily change the trajectory of your life. This is why it is vital to know which words spoken over you should be accepted or rejected. There are words that create vision, and juxtaposed to those words are words that kill vision. Maybe the vision is not dead, but if you are blind, you never recognize it.

It is imperative that every word be established. In saying that, we must also consider that none of us are infallible. In the body of Christ, we are all subject to make mistakes. As someone is growing in a gift, we are careful not to put them down but to help encourage and support them. So if we fall, we fall forward. Always cover one another with grace. When we bear with one another's weaknesses and undeveloped areas, we fulfill the law of Christ.

> If it is God's word, it can defend itself. Testing does not vilify, it validates.

When delivering a message, do not despise testing. This vetting process may feel uncomfortable at first, but remember, if it is God's word, it can defend itself. It is not to be considered a challenge but considered a confirmation. Testing does not vilify, it validates. Don't become emotionally involved with a word. We are not married to that word; we are married to Christ.

GREEN DROUGHT

In Ethiopia, there have been seasons of irregular rain causing green vegetation to rapidly appear. However, because of wrong timing, it has no nutritional value. This is called a "green drought."

> "The days are coming," declares the Sovereign LORD, "when I will send a famine through the land—not a famine of food or a thirst for water, but a famine of hearing the words of the LORD.
>
> AMOS 8:11 NIV

The beautiful green fields do not match the idea of what a drought should look like; nevertheless, people are starving, says the World Food Program.

Strange occurrences happen during "green droughts." Elephants have eaten their fill of lush green vegetation, only to die shortly thereafter. The nutritional value did not add up to the effort it took to eat. The end result is that an elephant can die of starvation with a full stomach. When people are hungry, they will eat anything. How miserable it must be to starve to death with a full stomach.

When God Confides in Man

> *The LORD confides in those who fear him; he makes his covenant known to them.*
>
> Psalm 25:14 NIV

When you are very close to someone, they may share a deep secret. They may even share a deep pain or struggle. But very few ever reach the most intimate place where the friend will become so vulnerable that they will show you their desire. These are the thoughts we hold close to our chest. We protect and preserve these most intimate thoughts so that we will not be embarrassed. No one wants to die at the hand of their own dreams.

But God is generous in revelation. He desires to show us His desires. Jesus said that it is the Spirit that coordinates this intimacy that changes the trajectory of our human existence. We move from existing because of Him to existing for Him.

> *"I no longer call you servants, because a servant does not know his master's business. Instead, I have called you friends, for everything that I learned from my Father I have made known to you."*
>
> John 15:15 NIV

When we ask the Holy Spirit to use us in the gifts He has given us, we will step in to our royal assignments. It is the kings who search out a matter.

As we face an era of confusion, I believe that God is raising up prophetic voices across the land. Voices of authenticity, not manipulation. Voices of power and demonstration. Voices not concerned with self-preservation or monetary gain. Voices that can't be bought because they are betrothed to another.

"Remember you are the donkey on Palm Sunday, never assume the applause is for you, it is for who you carry."

A.W. Tozer

Chapter 10

POWER ON
PERCEIVING THE SPIRIT: AVOIDING BLASPHEMY

PERCEPTION IS CRITICAL

Our perception of spiritual activity is critical in receiving supernatural power from the Holy Spirit. The New Testament Greek word *horáō* is translated "perceive" and defined by *HELPS Word Studies* "to see with the mind (i.e. spiritually see), perceive (with inward spiritual perception)." This is the word Jesus used when He rebuked the disciples for using natural reasoning (Matthew 16:9). It is also the word used for Peter's perception of Simon the Sorcerer's motives in wanting the ability to impart the Holy Spirit. While his request may have looked noble to the casual observer, his purpose was greed and personal exaltation, for which Peter rebuked him.

Supernatural perception is seeing deeper than the surface and is critical to spiritual understanding and collaboration with the Holy Spirit. If we perceive the Spirit's power at work, we can choose to recognize the supernatural activity as having its source in God and determine in our hearts to partner with Him. By this decision, we choose not to resist Him nor quench His flame within us. When we rightly perceive Him and follow His promptings, His supernatural power is unimpeded; He can flow through us as channels to accomplish His will on Earth. Conversely, we can decide *not* to acknowledge His presence and promptings. We may choose to resist His will and quench His Spirit. He is grieved by this, as He is looking for those whose hearts are fully devoted and yielded to Him; for these He will show Himself strong (2 Chronicles 16:9), revealing His supernatural power to and through them. It is a misperception to think you can ignore and resist Him on a continual basis without consequence. This may lead to a seared conscience or reprobate mind.

It is possible to see the Spirit at work, yet deliberately continue to hold onto preconceived ideas and misperceptions. This was the attitude of the Pharisees, the religious leaders of Jesus' day. When the Holy Spirit's power was at work, they stubbornly clung to their religious system and accused Christ of casting out devils by the power of Satan. They made a determined choice, refusing to acknowledge the power's source as coming from the Spirit of God through Jesus. They were warned in the strongest terms that their willful blindness could result in eternal unforgiveness and separation from God.

"Therefore I say to you, any sin and blasphemy shall be forgiven people, but blasphemy against the Spirit shall not be forgiven. Whoever speaks a word against the Son of Man, it shall be forgiven him; but whoever speaks against the Holy Spirit, it shall not be forgiven him, either in this age or in the age to come."

MATTHEW 12:31-32 NIV

WHAT IS BLASPHEMY?

Jesus warned that blasphemy against Himself and others can be forgiven, but blasphemy against the Holy Spirit will not. This is why it is called "the unpardonable sin." Knowing that the Father gave His only beloved Son and will forgive those who blaspheme Him, it is astounding that He will not forgive blasphemy of His Spirit. That makes it critical to understand and avoid.

So, what is blasphemy? Blasphemy means to show contempt, vilify, or speak evil of. Blasphemy is lack of reverence. It is insulting and degrading. *Thayer's Greek Lexicon* defines it as "slander, detraction, speech injurious to another's good name...reproachful speech injurious to the divine majesty."

In essence, blasphemy is to come against another, either by word or by deed. It is not accidental; it is deliberate. It is usually not a one-time offense but an aggregate measure of compounded violations.

We also blaspheme when we adapt to a lifestyle that has been rejected by the Holy Spirit. In fact, *HELPS Word Studies* further defines blasphemy this way:

> *Jesus warned that blasphemy against Himself and others can be forgiven, but blasphemy against the Holy Spirit will not.*

"blasphēmía (from *blax*, 'sluggish/slow,' and */phēmē*, 'reputation, fame')—blasphemy—literally, slow (sluggish) to call something good (that really is good)—and slow to identify what is truly bad (that really is evil). Blasphemy 'switches' right for wrong (wrong for right), i.e. calls what God disapproves, 'right' which 'exchanges the truth of God for a lie' (Rom. 1:25)."

Woe to those who call evil good and good evil, who put darkness for light and light for darkness, who put bitter for sweet and sweet for bitter.

Isaiah 5:20 NIV

THE SEARED CONSCIENCE

This is a process, as the apostle Paul explained to Timothy (1 Timothy 4:2). The example of a seared conscience illustrates the progression of corruption and its severe implications. When flesh has been seared or cauterized, it becomes void of feeling. In some cases, burn victims no longer have the ability to feel pain.

> *Leprosy kills nerve cells so that pain is no longer felt. In the same way, the sinner who habitually ignores the Spirit loses sensitivity until the conscience is seared past feeling.*

This process of searing the conscience was explained in "type" in the Old Testament laws concerning leprosy found in Leviticus 14. *The Cambridge Bible* notes, "leprosy had removed him who had been smitten [with leprosy] from the 'kingdom of priests'; that a reconsecration was necessary, before he could again take his place among his brethren. The leper was regarded (1) as one dead (see on Leviticus 13:45 f.), (2) as unclean, (3) as smitten of God: hence the ceremonial indicated (1) restoration to life, (2) removal of uncleanness, (3) readmission to God's presence." *(The Cambridge Bible, Leviticus 14 commentary, Biblehub.com, accessed June 6, 2017.)*

See that in all ways leprosy was symbolic of sin and its effect. This is why ceremonial cleansing was required before the leper could be restored to fellowship with the community and the worship of God.

In both the disease state of leprosy and the state of willful sin, the progression to numbness is gradual so that sensitivity is lost over a period of time. The disease kills nerve cells so that pain is no longer felt. It's said that as the fingers, toes, nose, and ears lose feeling and rot, the smell attracts rodents who eat the flesh while the leper sleeps. In the same way, the sinner who habitually ignores the Spirit loses sensitivity until the conscience is seared past feeling. Leprosy is a slow death by rotting the flesh; in the same way, sin corrupts the soul, ending in eternal spiritual death. The leper could suffer serious burns without being aware of it. This graphically illustrates the sinner, who no longer feels the pangs of conscience because of rejecting the Spirit and will experience the fire of judgment.

The Spirit strives to warn and convict, to spare of us this end; we ignore Him to our own peril. To insult, push away, and despise the One Who draws you to God and baptizes you into Christ is to leave yourself without hope of salvation. If we turn to Him, the Spirit of grace will give us power and victory over sin so that we can live in His Presence without judgment—that is the good news of the Gospel!

THE UNPARDONABLE SIN

This topic is of the utmost importance. Because the penalty of a violation of this magnitude is irreversible, this subject must be taken seriously. Understanding the unpardonable sin frightens the comfortable but comforts the frightened. Those who have lived in the fear produced by satanic tyranny will be comforted to know that they have been exonerated.

As believers, we should have a full understanding of what offends God to this measure of punishment. We cannot relax where God demands reverence. When the Scripture says "never forgiven," it literally means "never forgiven!" This judgment is unalterable, unchanging, and unrelenting. Stated plainly, it's terrifying.

STRONG WARNING

And so I tell you, every kind of sin and slander can be forgiven, but blasphemy against the Spirit will not be forgiven.
MATTHEW 12:31 NIV

This scripture begins with the assurance that every sin and blasphemy can be forgiven, "but".... So blasphemy can be forgiven but blasphemy against the Holy Spirit cannot.

Knowing the grace of God, it is difficult to wrap our minds around this eternal trespass. When reading Matthew 12:31-32, we hear a definitive severity in the tone of Jesus. When Jesus expounded on the topic of blasphemy against the Holy Ghost, He was not attempting to comfort those who had failed but to warn them of impending judgment - an irreversible punishment. The absence of tact or etiquette was due to the severity of the maximum penalty awarded. This was an austere warning, and for some this was a final warning! And that for all eternity!

Therefore consider the goodness and severity of God: on those who fell, severity; but toward you, goodness, if you continue in His goodness. Otherwise you also will be cut off.

ROMANS 11:22 NKJV

Understand this: God never brings judgment without warning. God is not a tyrant waiting to exact revenge upon His enemies. No, God is love. It is God's desire for all the world to be saved.

> *For I take no pleasure in the death of anyone, declares the Sovereign LORD. Repent and live!*
>
> Ezekiel 18:32 NIV

God has been committed to world salvation from the beginning. Some have falsely believed that God only loves them because Jesus died for them when, in fact, Jesus died for them because God loved them. God so loved them…that He gave, and gave, and gave. Knowing God's love and Christ's sacrifice, we must make a decision. We either accept or reject — there is no middle ground of indecisiveness.

Anyone who dies without God is in an unpardonable state. There are no "do-overs." Your fate, through disobedience, has been sealed for all eternity. There are no second chances after death.

> *Anyone who dies without God is in an unpardonable state. There are no "do-overs."*

In Mark chapter 3 we see the miraculous power of Jesus described. He goes from city to city, healing the sick, delivering the possessed, bringing hope to the oppressed. Many Pharisees followed Jesus from place to place attempting to build a case against Him. They sought for opportunities to accuse Him. As they witnessed His miracles, the only reasonable conclusion was that Jesus is God. The prideful Pharisees would not allow their spirit to be enlightened by truth; they stubbornly clung to a lie, willfully choosing to remain ignorant. (See 2 Peter 3:5; Romans 1:18-20.) Doggedly, they stalked and critiqued His every move. They were demonically inspired as they stood on the periphery gazing with disdain.

Jesus did not try to prove Himself or stoop to performance on their account. He refused to become their puppet by attempting to sway their erroneous opinions. Jesus remained obedient to the Father's desire.

Men of Israel, listen to this message: Jesus of Nazareth was a man certified by God to you by miracles, wonders, and signs, which God did among you through Him, as you yourselves know.

Acts 2:22 NIV

The compounding evidence was undeniable. Jesus was then, and is now, the Son of God! Although those with unclean spirits testified that Jesus was the Son of God, the Pharisees vehemently denied His Lordship. See His kindness in calling them to Himself in an attempt to help them perceive correctly and acknowledge the Holy Spirit's power at work through Him. But they would rather hold to their religious system and prideful positions than admit the truth.

The scribes who came down from Jerusalem were saying, "He is possessed by Beelzebul," and "He casts out the demons by the ruler of the demons." And He called them to Himself and began speaking to them in parables, "How can Satan cast out Satan?"

Mark 3:22-24 NIV

When the Pharisees attributed the work of God to Satan, Jesus drew the line. They are either dangerously close or have already given themselves over to this extreme violation. Jesus states that this sin can never be forgiven — not now, not ever!

Power On Perceiving the Spirit: Avoiding Blasphemy

"Truly I tell you, people can be forgiven all their sins and every slander they utter, but whoever blasphemes against the Holy Spirit will never be forgiven; they are guilty of an eternal sin."

MARK 3:28-29 NIV

If we deliberately keep on sinning after we have received the knowledge of the truth, no sacrifice for sins is left, but only a fearful expectation of judgment and of raging fire that will consume the enemies of God....How much more severely do you think someone deserves to be punished who has trampled the Son of God underfoot, who has treated as an unholy thing the blood of the covenant that sanctified them, and who has insulted the Spirit of grace? For we know him who said, "It is mine to avenge; I will repay," and again, "The Lord will judge his people." It is a dreadful thing to fall into the hands of the living God.

HEBREWS 10:26-31 NIV

WHO HAS BLASPHEMED?

First, we have all blasphemed. This may shock you but in your life's journey, you have spoken by word or acted irreverently towards something sacred, if not towards God Himself. This is by definition the act of blasphemy. The apostle Paul tells Timothy that he himself was a blasphemer.

Even though I was once a blasphemer and a persecutor and a violent man, I was shown mercy because I acted in ignorance and unbelief.

1 TIMOTHY 1:13 NIV

We cannot move forward by standing with a moral highbrow, unaware of our own actions. After all, our sins have insulted God. It is imperative that we come clean. We confess our transgressions. We own it for a moment, and then we move on. We repent and surrender to God.

The sins of some are obvious, reaching the place of judgment ahead of them; the sins of others trail behind them.

1 Timothy 5:24 NIV

You will never outrun your sin! We are quick to accuse others and quick to excuse ourselves. We all have the propensity for selective amnesia. You cannot outrun your iniquity; the only recourse is to confess and be released of your sin. When you repent, you are sending your sin ahead. Amazing imagery, but you actually allow your sin to outrun you to the judgment seat of God, where it is prejudged and reconciled by the efficacious sacrifice of Jesus. So sin's seat of judgment becomes your seat of mercy.

> When we confess sin, sin becomes impotent and powerless. Through repentance, the terror of our sin is shattered.

Imagine a race, in which your adversarial opponent is determined to get ahead of you. Now, this represents the beauty of confession. Unbeknownst to your archenemy, the bridge is out, so you let him pass. He's in first place, but you win! In other words, second place is the new first! It's counterintuitive — repentance never makes sense, it makes saints.

Unconfessed sin is unforgiven sin. What you expose, God will cover. What you cover, God will expose. When we confess sin, sin becomes impotent and powerless. We disarm sin of its cruel intentions, its dreadful memories, and gut-wrenching alarm. Through repentance, we humble ourselves, and the terror of our sin is shattered.

HAVE I COMMITTED BLASPHEMY AGAINST THE HOLY SPIRIT?

This is one of the most-asked questions on the internet. There is great fear concerning the danger of this unpardonable act, and rightly so.

In short, the answer is no. If you had committed the unpardonable sin, there would be absolutely no remorse or conscience left to even inquire about your eternal status. If you are disturbed in the least to imagine this, you have absolutely not committed this sin! Your conscience is still intact, not seared past feeling, as illustrated by the burn victim or the leper's condition. Now, this does not mean you haven't abused areas that need deliverance and healing, such as your mind and heart.

You see, the question itself produces the answer. The inquiry towards eternity is evidence of a heart that is still receiving communication from the Holy Spirit, even if that communication has been interrupted or numbed by trespass.

> *You see, the question itself produces the answer. The inquiry towards eternity is evidence of a heart that is still receiving communication from the Holy Spirit.*

Someone asked if it were possible to have accidentally committed this blasphemous act. The answer again is "no." Blasphemy of the Holy Spirit is not committed by accident! It is done willfully. Blasphemy of the Holy Spirit is an intentional, willful, rejection of God's Spirit. This is determined opposition. It is to disdain and show contempt towards the Holy Spirit, to an extreme place of no return. Sadly, in this state "the damned" are unwilling and unable to repent and believe.

Grieving the Spirit

And do not grieve the Holy Spirit of God, with whom you were sealed for the day of redemption.

Ephesians 4:30 NIV

> When we offend the Spirit, He is deeply saddened, experiences pain, and grieves, not because He is petty... He carries a burden for our eternal souls.

When we knowingly walk in disobedience, we grieve the Holy Spirit. The Spirit is a divine person with strong emotions. *HELPS Word Studies* defines the Greek word translated "grieve" as meaning "to experience deep, emotional pain (sadness), i.e. severe sorrow (grief). [The Greek word] *lypeō* is very intense and hence even used of the pain of childbirth (see Gen 3:16)."

The depth of feeling can be known by understanding that this is the same word used for the grief experienced when a loved one dies. When we offend the Spirit, He is deeply saddened, experiences pain, and grieves for us; not because He is petty but because He is holy. He carries a burden for our eternal souls.

Some actions that grieve the Spirit are impure speech, lying, sexual immorality, anger, brawling, bitterness, and unforgiveness. These offenses can be acted out in thought or in deed.

Yet they rebelled and grieved his Holy Spirit. So he turned and became their enemy and he himself fought against them.

Isaiah 63:10 NIV

Quenching the Spirit

Do not quench the Spirit.

1 Thessalonians 5:19

Quenching the Spirit is by no means controlling the Spirit. It is a willful decision that God has allowed you to have. In essence, God allows us, or permits us, to resist His Spirit. In placing free will in our hands, when we turn to Him our pursuit is genuine, not mechanical or forced.

To quench the Spirit is to despise or show contempt towards the Spirit. Definitions of this Greek word *shennumi* include extinguish, quench, suppress, thwart, and stifle. It is sobering to think that mere human beings can thwart the purposes of God by quenching His Spirit. This can be forgiven but should be considered more than a misdemeanor. This is a critical decision that can lead to full-blown blasphemy.

Quenching or suppressing the Spirit is a dangerous position to be in. You become judge to the Judge. How could that ever end well?

To quench also refers to a fire being extinguished. The Holy Spirit is a fire on the inside of us. He burns with passion for God. When our thoughts become polluted with carnality, we offer nothing to the fire; we suppress, stifle, and extinguish it. Fire must be fed to stay alive.

Without wood a fire goes out...

Proverbs 26:20a NIV

Supernatural Power on Earth

Paul exhorts Timothy to do just the opposite.

For this reason I remind you to fan into flame the gift of God, which is in you through the laying on of my hands.

2 TIMOTHY 1:6 NIV

We should, as Paul said, fan into flame the Spirit rather than suppress or quench the Spirit.

RESISTING THE SPIRIT

Resistance describes an attitude or action that is not receptive. Resistance opposes what has been presented. It is in essence "anti." Those who are resistant are not easily moved or influenced. The verse quoted below is the only place in the Bible where it occurs. We can see how seriously the Spirit perceives this offense when we understand the Greek definition: "to fall against (contrary); actively (aggressively) resisting, like someone trying to crush an adversary in battle" *(HELPS Word Studies)*.

You stiff-necked people! Your hearts and ears are still uncircumcised. You are just like your ancestors: You always resist the Holy Spirit!

ACTS 7:51 NIV

Stephen, the first Christian martyr, was facing the hostility of unbelievers when he spoke the words quoted above. Many of the people of Israel had completely rejected the Spirit, as they'd had opportunity to hear and believe. They were judgmental, lacking self-awareness, and ignorant of God's grace. And for some, this would be their last opportunity for redemption, but they chose resistance instead.

In Stephen's discourse, he gives his antagonists historical data as evidence that resistance had begun with their fathers. Their rejection of the Sprit was a generational downward spiral, and they would soon share the same fate as their defiant fathers.

> *It is a dangerous thing to reject what the Spirit has revealed.*

The Holy Spirit convicts the world of sin and convinces us of righteousness and God's judgment. The Spirit was speaking through Stephen. Sadly, as Stephen was being rejected, the Holy Spirit Himself was being rejected.

It is a dangerous thing to reject what the Spirit has revealed. While occupying earth, we still have choices. Our life is the evidence of what we choose and refuse.

DISTANCE A DETERMINED DECISION

Being close to God has always been our choice. God said if we would draw near to Him, He would always draw near to us.

"Everywhere is within walking distance if you have the time."

Steven Wright

The Holy Spirit makes every effort to convict, to convince, and to contend for our hearts. It is the Spirit that tugs at your heart for closeness. When we reject the Spirit, we are rejecting God.

Where can I go from your Spirit? Where can I flee from your presence?

Psalms 139:7 NIV

A Codependent Hermit

In the book, *The Stranger in the Woods: The Extraordinary Story of the Last True Hermit* (New York: Alfred A. Knopf, a division of Penguin Random House LLC, 2017), author Michael Finkel chronicled the journey of Christopher Knight, "the north pond hermit."

In 1986, at twenty years of age, Christopher Thomas Knight drove his Subaru from his home in Massachusetts to the deep forests of Maine. He weaved his car as far into the woods as he could. With no premeditation, he walked deep into the woods. Unprepared, unconcerned, he just kept walking. Is he careless or carefree? Time will tell.

He claimed to have never built a fire as he nestled deep into the dense forest. In thick brush and between huge boulders, he burrowed in seclusion. For 27 winters, he battled the elements. No communication with the outside world. No microwave, no plumbing, no internet.

He was largely undetected for nearly three decades, robbing the neighboring communities of the strangest items. He became the subject of folklore as propane tanks, batteries, tarps, and snacks were pilfered. It was estimated that he committed over a thousand burglaries. Just small, mostly insignificant things missing here and there, but not worth the pursuit of the thief.

Some local communities were more suspicious than others, but it would always die down. Although many believed the tales of the hermit from Maine, no one ever came close to discovering his secret until the night he was caught breaking into the pantry of a nearby camp for the handicapped.

He defied logic with his self-sustaining will to go it alone. He was not a fugitive or a victim of a traumatic event. He just wanted to be left alone.

In Genesis 2:18, God reveals the first human dilemma. It is not Satan or his schemes — it is aloneness. God said, "Man is alone, and it is not good." The first thing God calls "not good" is not sin but aloneness.

God sets the lonely in families, he leads out the prisoners with singing; but the rebellious live in a sun-scorched land.

PSALMS 68:6 NIV

Christopher Knight is an allegory of modern man's humanistic efforts to find peace and solitude. For humankind, there is no peace outside of God's presence.

Christopher may have had a very high idea of self-dependency but was reduced to becoming a petty thief, if only to supply his basic needs. He really couldn't do it alone! None of us can. His makeshift bunker was littered with candy and chip wrappers. He had survived aided by junk food he stole from neighboring children's camps.

No doctors, no dentist, no teeth. For nearly three decades the junk food had taken its toll. How he endured those years is an incredible feat of human will and perseverance, but it all came to an abrupt end because he needed help.

Although distance is a decision, it is a bad decision. No matter how highly we value our will, we will always need help.

"He who created us without our help will not save us without our consent."

SAINT AUGUSTINE

INTOLERANT OF THE DISTANCE BETWEEN US

If you are reading this and feel you or someone you know have drifted too far, you haven't. The Spirit Himself draws near to you. Your

> The Spirit Himself draws near to you. Your questions alone are proof your spirit is still teachable.

questions alone are proof your spirit is still teachable. You have not resisted beyond rescue.

I once kept a blind deer. He was a rescue deer, so we gave him a home, fed him, and protected him. I would often sneak to the barn, walking barefoot as quietly as I possibly could. Knowing deer have a keen sense of smell, I would slip in downwind. As I would stealthily try to approach him, he would immediately stand to his feet and face me head on. He just knew. When someone is close, you just know.

Spirit-led people do not require a lot of natural evidence. Their confirmation comes from within. The Holy Spirit is their internal witness. I believe that you have been given opportunities to encounter the Spirit. You know. Even if you've tried to convince yourself otherwise, you know. Like truth, He's been there, maybe in the shadows or misrepresented perhaps, but in reality, you know.

He Himself has said, "I WILL NEVER DESERT YOU, NOR WILL I EVER FORSAKE YOU..."

Hebrews 13:5b NASB

Chapter 11

POWER ON
GLOBAL SALVATION

It will come about after this that I will pour out My Spirit on all mankind; and your sons and daughters will prophesy, your old men will dream dreams, your young men will see visions. Even on the male and female servants I will pour out My Spirit in those days.

JOEL 2:28-29 NIV

The foundation of your spiritual walk begins with the Holy Spirit. The Holy Spirit is the person of the Godhead Who is in action on the earth today. Often called "the Matchmaker," it is Him Who introduces us to and calls us to Christ. The Holy Spirit causes us to love and magnify God. He instills a desire for God's Word, a sensitivity towards sin, and a receptivity to change. He has been sent to bring the whole world to salvation. His indwelling presence woos mankind to seek a relationship with Christ. His infilling transforms man from the inside out. He is the supernatural power of God on Earth.

FOR ALL WHO THIRST

Now on the last day, the great day of the feast, Jesus stood and cried out, saying, "If anyone is thirsty, let him come to Me and drink. He who believes in Me, as the Scripture said, 'From his innermost being will flow rivers of living water.'" But this He spoke of the Spirit, whom those who believed in Him were to receive; for the Spirit was not yet given, because Jesus was not yet glorified.

JOHN 7:37-39 NIV

The setting was the Feast of Tabernacles (Sukkoth). This feast is also called the "ingathering," which is significant in relation to global salvation.

On the eighth day, referred to as the "great day," the priest would go to the pool of Siloam. The priest would then fill a large golden pitcher with water and one with wine (each symbols of the Spirit). This water libation ceremony commemorated the prophecy of Isaiah. The priest would then draw water from the pool of Siloam (meaning "sent") and bring the vessels through the water gates to offer at the temple altar.

With joy you will draw water from the wells of salvation.

ISAIAH 12:3 NIV

The ceremony was full of type and imagery. The people participating in the ceremony knew the customs, but soon they would be privy to a new revelation. The ceremony was to give God thanks for the previous year's provision and to ask God for the coming year's rain for the crops. Of course, rain was vital for the preservation of life.

Jesus asks, "Is anyone thirsty?" He was not making an appeal for the earth's desperate need for water but for man's desperate need for the Spirit. As rain would fall to nourish the harvest, so would God's Spirit fall upon every man who would receive. The Spirit is the essential water that sustains life.

> Jesus asks, "Is anyone thirsty?" The Spirit is the essential water that sustains life.

In the libation ceremony, the priest would pour the water over the four horns of the altar. To the Jew, this symbolic act of spilling water represented rainfall and the hope of water tables to be filled to capacity. But the greater meaning was misinterpreted. This act symbolically represented a deluge of God's Spirit over the whole world. Jesus conveyed the true meaning as water was generously poured over the altar. This act was in anticipation of the Spirit's supernatural, global outpouring.

John reiterated this when he wrote, "and this spoke He of the Spirit." This was an illustrated truth that God's Spirit would flow and saturate the earth, that world evangelism was on its way!

Uncommon to the character of Jesus, He cries in a loud voice, "Is anyone thirsty?" There is an urgency to see the world saved. In the broad view of global salvation, we must always take seriously the prospect of eternity without God, that is, eternity in Hell. With this in mind, it should always be our position to do all we can with all we have while we have the opportunity to save the lost.

"Life's most persistent and urgent question is, 'What are you doing for others?'"
MARTIN LUTHER KING, JR., SERMON
"THREE DIMENSIONS OF A COMPLETE LIFE"
FROM THE 1963 COLLECTION *STRENGTH TO LOVE*

NOT FOR DEBATE

> *So Paul stood in the midst of the Areopagus and said, "Men of Athens, I observe that you are very religious in all respects. For while I was passing through and examining the objects of your worship, I also found an altar with this inscription, 'TO AN UNKNOWN GOD.' Therefore what you worship in ignorance, this I proclaim to you."*
>
> ACTS 17:22-23 NIV

As he walks through Athens, the apostle Paul is disturbed to find a city immersed in idolatry. These are not uneducated, ignorant people but the academically elite. They are renowned for their intellectualism and willingness to be open-minded. They are charismatic and extremely liberal. They are devoted to science, literature, and opulent luxury. Ironically, America resembles this early culture with our education, entertainment, sexual perversion, and moral liberality.

This is Paul's second missionary journey. He is determined to preach the gospel to the whole world. Opportunity has a shelf life. The opportunity of a lifetime must be seized during the lifetime of that opportunity. We must "strike while the iron is hot."

> The opportunity of a lifetime must be seized during the lifetime of that opportunity.

Daily the apostle Paul would lay down the framework of his message in the synagogue and then proceed to the marketplace. Like Jesus, he would go to where they were. His plea was more than a call to repentance, it was a command to repentance.

As he encountered the Epicurean and Stoic philosophers, he incited their interest with his thought-provoking arguments. These men then led him to the epicenter of thought and deliberation, Mars Hill. Men of renown like Plato, Aristotle, and Socrates would call this home. Mars Hill was the place to be if you were a statesman, poet, or sage. This was intellectual networking at its best.

Mars Hill was also the meeting place for the Areopagus Court. This court was similar to our Supreme Court. Here they judged and settled civil, criminal, and religious matters. Significantly, during this time the Areopagus was the most prominent place for philosophy, religion, and law in the whole world.

At Mars Hill, Paul would give one of the most prolific messages recorded in Scripture. He immediately exploited the wrong view of God that they held due to their ignorance. If you can imagine, Paul is before the most learned men in the world, systematically revealing their ignorance and depravity. It is amazing how those striving for excellence will often settle for ignorance.

> *It is amazing how those striving for excellence will often settle for ignorance.*

Paul, the apologist, shows great poise as he reveals their lack of knowledge in serving "dumb idols." The crowd is speechless as Paul points out their futile worship to the "unknown god."

Paul's approach is not mean, it's meaningful. Although convincing, Paul is not bullish. He is not trying to win an argument; he's trying to win the world.

He defends the God of the universe, the true God that *can be known* by His children. He politely and tactfully persuades them to interrogate their own erroneous belief system. He provokes them to reason amongst themselves, but many of the Greeks considered his words "folly." Even a man as profound as Paul is rejected when hearts are hardened to the message.

Without trepidation, Paul draws attention to the certainty and urgency of the truth. He passionately compares and contrasts the views of the surrounding Jewish and gentile world. He even takes on racism as he proclaims, "all men are made of one blood."

His message is powerful and informative. It is instructional so that any could believe, but we have no record of a great response. We are told only a few believed. There is no ground-sweeping evidence of a great revival, no mass conversions, no churches planted, only a few who believed, and some who mocked. We know that God's word never returns void, but for the most part, their exemplary display of prolific intellect rewarded Paul with little or no change. In essence, the missionary campaign to Athens appeared to be unsuccessful and anti-climactic.

The Game Changer

Don't tell me what I can't do, let me show you what I can do!

I can do all things through Christ which strengthens me.

Philippians 4:13 NKJV

Paul departs from Athens after great rejection. He is still determined to share the gospel throughout Greece. He turns to the neighboring city of Corinth. Here we truly see the genius of the apostle Paul. This is not displayed in the form of who he is but in Whose he is. Not from his intellect, education, or pedigree, but from his spirit and desire to be faithful at the expense of self. Juxtaposed to Mars Hill, Paul's approach will be drastically modified.

With Paul's skill set, he can do whatever needs to be done. He never lacks confidence or readiness. He is sincere and passionate in every effort, ready to promote the gospel, ready to perform his duty. But this time it's different. This speaks of more than the willingness to go; it speaks of the wisdom to wait — that is, to wait on the Spirit!

Until the Spirit is poured on us from on high, and the desert becomes a fertile field, and the fertile field seems like a forest.

ISAIAH 32:15 NIV

Listen to the newly revised apostle Paul. He pivots away from the effort and knowledge of man, and towards humility and dependency upon the Spirit.

And when I came to you, brethren, I did not come with superiority of speech or of wisdom, proclaiming to you the testimony of God. For I determined to know nothing among you except Jesus Christ, and Him crucified.

1 CORINTHIANS 2:1-2 NIV

Determined to know nothing? Wait — you, Paul? You're brilliant! Know nothing? How difficult it must have been for this accomplished, exceptional man to know nothing. Paul was determined to see a different outcome than before.

[A]nd my message and my preaching were not in persuasive words of wisdom, but in demonstration of the Spirit and of power, so that your faith would not rest on the wisdom of men, but on the power of God.

1 CORINTHIANS 2:4-5 NIV

Although Corinth was known as a seat of sensuality and immorality, the apostle Paul found renewed hope and vision. The Holy Spirit testified to the restorative power of God. A church was founded by Paul and many souls transformed.

Supernatural Power on Earth

> *"Not by might nor by power, but by my Spirit," says the LORD Almighty.*
>
> ZECHARIAH 4:6B NIV

The church in Corinth had an abundance of difficulties, but they were continually taking ground in a godless society. The end result was success; the Kingdom was advancing. If you've been keeping score, there are two books in the Bible that carry the name Corinthians; there is no book in the Bible titled "Mars Hill."

> Head knowledge can only speak to head knowledge. Spirit speaks to spirit.

Head knowledge can only speak to head knowledge. Spirit speaks to spirit. The apostle Paul said in Romans 7:18, "in my flesh dwells no good thing." This is why Paul made a quick audible when entering the contemporary, commercial city of Corinth. From here on, the Spirit would set Paul's itinerary. He will no longer rely on homiletical skills or his privileged education. He does not change his message; he changes his method. He puts total confidence in the Spirit for bringing salvation to the unredeemed city. Flesh would not and could not get the results needed to save the Corinthians.

> *And my message and my preaching were not in persuasive words of wisdom [using clever rhetoric], but [they were delivered] in demonstration of the [Holy] Spirit [operating through me] and of [His] power [stirring the minds of the listeners and persuading them], so that your faith would not rest on the wisdom and rhetoric of men, but on the power of God.*
>
> 1 CORINTHIANS 2:4-5 AMP

It is the Spirit that transforms lives! We need this encounter with the fire of God.

"If you want to get warm, you move near the fire."

C.S. Lewis, *Mere Christianity*

Empowered By His Spirit

But you will receive power when the Holy Spirit comes on you; and you will be my witnesses in Jerusalem, and in all Judea and Samaria, and to the ends of the earth.

Acts 1:8 NIV

The promise of the infilling of the Holy Spirit would be the proof that the Kingdom had not failed at the crucifixion of Jesus. The promise was the assurance that the world could be saved.

The Spirit would usher in a new thrust of power for global evangelization. The uttermost parts of the earth would feel the effects of this outpouring. The demonstration of strength and power would propel the disciples forward with new boldness to face any challenge, even if it cost them their lives. And for some, it did.

"Father, teach us to give, and not to count the cost."

Excerpt from Prayer of St. Ignatius of Loyola

The Holy Spirit would enable the disciples to preach the gospel with power, followed by miracles that confirmed their words. He would give them courage to face persecution head on without wavering. The Holy Spirit would guide them through journeys of travail and opposition, enabled by power from another world. The disciples' journeys would require supernatural power that they were unfamiliar with. They had witnessed this power in Jesus; now they too would be conduits of this glory. This would only be available after the Holy Ghost had come upon them. The Holy Spirit was the prerequisite for this power and authority.

They would be commissioned to go to Jerusalem, the very place Jesus had been crucified. They were sent to Judea, a distinct land with its own peculiarities. And to Samaria, the forbidden place, a place of dishonor and racial tension. And then to the whole world.

Because of the Spirit, there is hope for the world. Global salvation is more than possible, it's probable.

And hope does not put us to shame, because God's love has been poured out into our hearts through the Holy Spirit, who has been given to us.
ROMANS 5:5 NIV

QUIT TALKING, BEGIN DOING

When God's love is shed abroad in our hearts we stand in awe. Confused that we could be counted worthy, but by His Spirit, convinced that we are! Dark becomes light. We are illuminated by this flame of incandescent love and affirmation. By His Spirit, we are unstoppable! The mandate is clear: Populate Heaven, pillage Hell!

> Belief is backed by behavior!

You are the living epistle read by men (2 Corinthians 3:2). People won't read your Bible, but they will read you. They watch you daily, whether you're aware of it or not. Belief is backed by behavior! We must be led by the Spirit as we navigate our way through this hostile world.

Today, you too can answer the high call. Ask the Spirit for guidance and direction. Begin now. Logistically, there are so many people in the world that cannot be reached unless you answer the call. Exercise your power in the Holy Ghost. Become a mouthpiece for God today. We know that there are 7 days in a week but someday is not one of them.

"The price of greatness is responsibility."

WINSTON CHURCHILL, QUOTATION FROM A SPEECH
GIVEN BY THE BRITISH PRIME MINISTER
HARVARD UNIVERSITY, SEPTEMBER 6 1943

Chapter 12

POWER ON
PROGRESSIVE REVELATION

THE DOVE

The dove has always been one of the purest depictions of the Holy Spirit. Through progressive revelation in the Bible, we clearly see the ways and nuances of the Spirit through the imagery of the dove. Like any sign, the dove is a visible representation that points to something; in this case, something deeper in the Spirit.

Doves are white, which represents goodness and purity.

Doves are never in a predictable pattern; they are constantly moving. The Spirit is always on the move, never dull or sedentary.

The dove is a clean bird, extremely cautious and selective in its diet. It's not content to eat just anything. The Spirit is also selective. All can receive, but the Spirit is partial to those who value purity.

The dove is a bird that communicates, but you must be still to hear it. Doves mysteriously enter and exit a place unannounced. Does this sound familiar?

The dove's gentleness and quietness reminds us of the Spirit's humility; He refuses to speak of himself, deflecting attention towards Christ. The dove is never proud or flamboyant, but He is exceptionally beautiful. He never puts on a show. His movements are deliberate and calculated, always with a purpose.

The dove comes from above to rest upon the earth. The Holy Spirit was sent from above to the people of the earth. We do not bring Earth to Him; He brings Heaven to us.

Jesus recognized the innocent character of the dove as He commissioned the disciples to face a hostile world. We do not normally associate innocence with boldness, but this is what is clearly seen here.

"Behold, I am sending you out as sheep, in the midst of wolves, so be wise as serpents and innocent as doves."

MATTHEW 10:16 NIV

We must live above reproach, placing a demand for innocence upon our own lives, lest we bring shame to the cause of Christ. The greater the purity in our lives, the greater the power in our lives.

THE LAW OF FIRST MENTION

In biblical theology there is a concept called the "law of first mention." Basically, when something is mentioned for the first time in the Bible, the essence of that person or thing is expressed in that first reference. According to this principle, we learn much about something upon first introduction. The theme is then predetermined for that person, place, or thing throughout the entirety of Scripture.

For example, a serpent in Genesis 3 became the symbol of Satan or demons. A lamb in Exodus 12 became identified with Christ, God's sacrifice.

Now the earth was formless and empty, darkness was over the surface of the deep, and the Spirit of God was hovering over the waters.

GENESIS 1:2 NIV

The first mention of the Holy Spirit was that of brooding or hovering over the waters. This would establish the essence of the Spirit's covering, His watching over us like a hen brooding over her chicks. He is fluid, constantly in motion, dynamic, and never static. He is mysterious, yet protectively engaged. The Spirit is constantly and consistently on guard.

> *The Spirit watches over us like a hen over her chicks. He is constantly and consistently on guard.*

The Holy Spirit is the First Responder. We recognize His hovering over the formless void; we understand that when we were incomplete, dark, and chaotic, He was patiently brooding over us.

THE ARK

The first mention in Scripture of a dove is in the deluge narrative. In Genesis 6, we see the judgment of God upon Earth's people who have utterly rejected Him. Their thoughts were on evil continually. God warned Noah and sent a flood to purge the world of this evil.

Fortunately, Noah found grace in the eyes of the Lord. God would use Noah to build a floating zoo to perpetuate life. Noah would carry more than family and animals to safety; he would carry God's favor and promises for mankind.

The Ark was a type and shadow of the Trinity. It had three floors, symbolic of the Father, the Son, and the Holy Ghost.

The ark only had one door. This was an exclusive entrance. Jesus said "I Am the Door, if anyone enters by Me he will be saved." There is no other way to enter the Kingdom. It has been erroneously said, "All roads lead to God." This is false, but all roads can lead to Jesus. He can rescue us no matter what road we're presently travelling. Still, there is only one road (one door) that leads to God and that is Jesus.

The ark was sealed with pitch. This tar-like substance was used to waterproof the floating stockyard. The imagery is congruent with the seal of God that preserves us by His Spirit (Ephesians 1:13).

The ark had a window in the top. No doubt, there was an awning or door to protect the window from the elements.

> *For promotion cometh neither from the east, nor from the west, nor from the south.*
> PSALM 75:6 KJV

Promotion comes from above! The meaning is to simply "look up"—your help comes from above. God is in charge, the highest of heavens belong to the Lord.

As the waters began to recede, Noah sends two birds out. These were used as indicators to find land. Although they were both birds, the raven and the dove were extremely different. They didn't look the same, eat the same, or behave the same.

THE RAVEN

The raven was sent out first. Obviously, he found what he was looking for because he never returned. The raven is comparable to the buzzard. He will eat anything; he especially enjoys dead flesh.

In the Bible, "flesh" is the term designated for the lower, sinful nature of man. The word "carnal" comes from the Latin word *carnis*, which means "flesh." The carnal flesh is ruled by basic physical, unregenerate lusts and desires. In Mark 4:4, ravens symbolize demonic hosts. They are unclean birds, preying upon flesh, disrupting the life-giving word. (We have all inherited this flesh nature through our father Adam. Grace allows us to survive our weakness but never supports our weakness. The good news is, God did more through Jesus than we ever did through Adam.)

From his overhead window, Noah watches the scavenger in flight. The raven flies back and forth. From his vantage point, this is all Noah observes, but the raven can't fly back and forth forever. Nothing can sustain that much effort without rest. Evidently, he found a place to rest. It wasn't dry ground — it had to be something or someone floating.

So Noah only sees the raven's flight pattern over the flooded Earth. Can you imagine the masses of dead flesh floating just above the tops of the submerged mountains? Surely, this was the resting place for the raven. No doubt, without a place to land, he could rest upon the buoyant carnage. We can never become comfortable with flesh. This is a type and shadow of uncontested immorality.

For those who are according to the flesh set their minds on the things of the flesh, but those who are according to the Spirit, the things of the Spirit. For the mind set on the flesh is death, but the mind set on the Spirit is life and peace

ROMANS 8:5-6 NIV

THE DOVE FINDS THE RESTING PLACE

Noah releases the dove three times. The deluge has ended, so Noah must investigate to see how far the waters have receded. Noah sends the dove out on an exploratory mission. The dove is to navigate the saturated terrain and direct towards dry ground.

[A]nd he sent out a raven, and it flew here and there until the water was dried up from the earth. Then he sent out a dove from him, to see if the water was abated from the face of the land;

but the dove found no resting place for the sole of her foot, so she returned to him into the ark, for the water was on the surface of all the earth. Then he put out his hand and took her, and brought her into the ark to himself.

GENESIS 8:7-9 NIV

As Noah's family is anxious to disembark the floating zoo, the dove will be the determining factor on whether to exit or to delay. The dove will be the sign to disembark or continue waiting.

> The Holy Spirit is necessary upon entrances and exits in our lives.

The Holy Spirit is necessary upon entrances and exits in our lives; He begins and ends seasons of our lives. He, the Spirit, turns the page.

On its first mission, the dove finds no place to rest, so she returns to the ark. This is indicative of a generation that has rejected the Spirit. Even self-proclaimed houses of God have decided the Spirit is unnecessary in this modern era. So like the dove, He finds no rest there.

Unlike the raven, the dove was more selective. The dove is a clean bird; her diet consists mostly of seeds. A dove will not rest on a carcass of dead flesh. The dove came back to the ark refusing to light upon the dead.

The Holy Spirit, like the dove refuses to rest where flesh surfaces. Keeping the law of first mention in mind, this has always been the position of the Spirit. The Spirit and the flesh are contrary one to the other.

Flesh gives birth to flesh, but the Spirit gives birth to spirit.

JOHN 3:6 NIV

On its second release, the dove brought back an olive branch. This was a significant find; now, Noah knew the earth was beginning to surface from its blue abyss. Life had begun to spring forth. The dove and the olive branch is an image used still today to represent peace.

The third time the dove was sent out, it never returned. This was the sign Noah had been looking for. Now it was safe to leave the ark. But where is the dove? Are we willing to search for Him? Has He found a place to rest?

Now arise, LORD God, and come to your resting place, you and the ark of your might. May your priests, LORD God, be clothed with salvation, may your faithful people rejoice in your goodness.

ISAIAH 11:10 NIV

Combining the three instances when Noah released it from the ark, we see the dove was selective, the dove was a symbol of peace, and the dove represented safety.

> When truth has been compromised, the Holy Spirit withdraws Himself.

From Noah until now, like the dove, the Spirit is searching for life, refusing to collaborate with dead flesh. The dove represents the Spirit of truth. When truth has been compromised, the Holy Spirit withdraws Himself.

THE MYSTERIOUSLY BEAUTIFUL ONE

The Song of Solomon is full of imagery that celebrates love. It is a prophetic parallel in which the young man represents Christ and the young maiden represents His love, the church. It is straightforward in its descriptions of married love. It is not lewd, though extremely sensual. It is raw and earthy.

Tucked within the pages of the song is another example of the dove, which represents the Spirit.

How beautiful you are, my darling! Oh, how beautiful! Your eyes are doves.

SONG OF SOLOMON 1:15 NIV

Solomon uses the dove as a symbol of beauty. The Holy Spirit, like the dove, is an object of beauty.

The most precious things in life are never held in our hands, but held in our hearts. Physical beauty has always been measured with the eyes; this is a false measure for true beauty. True beauty is not concerned with the container but with the contents inside.

It is possible to lose sight of the beauty of the Spirit when distracted by the blessings of the Spirit. When we seek His hand and not His face, we become obsessed with the gift instead of the Giver. The Holy Spirit is beautiful and leaves His residue over whatever He touches.

My dove in the clefts of the rock, in the hiding places on the mountainside, show me your face, let me hear your voice; for your voice is sweet, and your face is lovely.

SONG OF SOLOMON 2:14 NIV

Here we see the alluring aspect of the dove. The dove is in hiding. This is not to go unseen but to entice the search. God wants to be wanted!

We are amazed at His work, we are thankful for His presence, but we sometimes neglect His beauty. He is more than all-powerful, all-knowing, and omnipresent — He is beautiful.

Power On Progressive Revelation

Abandon your towns and dwell among the rocks, you who live in Moab. Be like a dove that makes its nest at the mouth of a cave.

JEREMIAH 48:28 NIV

Again, we see the imagery of a dove in hiding. His way of seeming aloof is actually to attract and allure interest. Like a love game, this is only to draw you in. There has always been a hiding in the nature of God.

Truly you are a God who has been hiding himself, the God and Savior of Israel.

ISAIAH 45:15 NIV

This ambiguous affection is not always understood. For this reason some lose interest, while others pursue and discover intimacy readily available.

I remember when things in my life began to emotionally evolve with a girl named Bobbi I met in college (now my wife). I began to notice where she was and where she wasn't. I continually monitored the walking paths that wound throughout our small campus. I gazed through crowds discreetly, subconsciously hoping to find her somewhere. Every day I felt motivated to find her. What was she wearing? Who was she with?

I felt torn and tormented by love. I did and didn't like the feelings I was experiencing. Simultaneously, I felt very alive while extremely uncertain and vulnerable. I needed to see her daily, even if that meant just a glimpse.

Finally, she made a few subtle gestures that invited me into her mystery. She played cool for a long time and left me guessing, but when she gave me the nod, I was never the same. Smitten!

> The Spirit is not low-hanging fruit that we should commonly feel entitled to.

The Spirit invites us in to His mystery so that He can reveal His majesty. The beauty of God should never be taken for granted. The Spirit is precious and uniquely special. The Spirit is not low-hanging fruit that we should commonly feel entitled to. He is magnificent and we should always recognize His overwhelming beauty. He is "top shelf" — we should always reach for Him with desire and desperation.

O worship the LORD in the beauty of holiness: fear before him, all the earth.

Psalm 96:9 KJV

THE DOVE'S APPEARANCE AT THE BAPTISM

Prior to His earthly ministry, Jesus went to the Jordan River to be baptized by John the Baptist. This would fulfill all righteousness and be a miraculous sign of Christ's divinity. At Jesus' baptism (Mark 1:10) the Spirit descended upon Him in the likeness of, and none other than, a dove.

After being baptized, Jesus came up immediately from the water; and behold, the heavens were opened, and he saw the Spirit of God descending as a dove and lighting on Him, and behold, a

voice out of the heavens said, "This is My beloved Son, in whom I am well-pleased."

Matthew 3:16-17 NIV

As Jesus came up from the water the Holy Spirit, like a dove, descended upon Him. Then the heavens were opened, and the Father's voice of affirmation followed. This rite of passage will set Jesus as the prototype for the Spirit-filled life.

Doves were seen in the ancient world as representatives of the divine. Doves were also symbols of love. God declared at the baptism that Jesus was His "beloved" Son. He also declared His love for us, when He gave His Son to remove our sin.

What came in the appearance of a dove was the Holy Spirit. The Holy Spirit is just that, a spirit. But on this occasion the Spirit appeared in a bodily shape like a dove. The Spirit is like the wind; we cannot see it, we only see the effects of the wind. The Spirit is not visible to us. On this particular occasion, the Spirit took on a form to be an emblem of peace, and a confirmation of Christ's deity.

The dove stayed. Unlike the dove in Noah's day, this dove remained on Jesus.

For the one whom God has sent [Jesus] speaks the words of God, for God gives [him] the Spirit without limit.

John 3:34 NIV

The Dove is Released

To be released implies that the dove must have previously been bound.

Temple worship was a necessary part of the Jewish custom. According to Jewish law, every man must pay a tribute of a half shekel upon arrival at the temple. This was Jewish currency; however, the Romans were in control of the Jewish state, so money had to be exchanged into Roman coin. This presented a great opportunity for manipulation, as money changers and sellers of merchandise flooded the streets of Jerusalem. Thousands of people came to the Feasts in Jerusalem, so fraud and usury were very common. Rest assured, wherever there's a crowd, there's a counterfeit.

Like an entry fee, two doves or pigeons were required for sacrifice before entering the temple according to Levitical law. The bird business had become quite lucrative. People travelled from far away to come to Jerusalem, so it became convenient to have these items for sale on location. Here comes the shakedown. The temple had become the place where sellers could gouge the worshipers and charge ridiculous prices. Again, this created opportunity for exploitation and manipulation.

After the first miracle of Jesus (water into wine), Jesus participates in the Passover feast in Jerusalem. This will be the first "cleansing of the temple" by Jesus. As Jesus witnesses the extortion in His house, he began to braid cords together to form a whip. This is not blind rage. This is premeditated justice; this is righteous indignation. Jesus was disgusted at what had become of the house of prayer. He is not concerned for self-preservation as He boldly and forcefully drives the perpetrators out. He overturns the tables of the money changers and releases the caged birds.

> Be careful not to release what God wants caged and not to cage what God wants released.

When Jesus enters the temple, the dove is set free. Be careful not to release what God wants caged and not to cage what God wants released.

And He made a scourge of cords, and drove them all out of the temple, with the sheep and the oxen; and He poured out the coins of the money changers and overturned their tables; and to those who were selling the doves He said, "Take these things away; stop making My Father's house a place of business."

JOHN 2: 15-16 NIV

This occurred at the beginning of Jesus' public ministry. This happens again at the end of His public ministry on Earth. Three years later, just after His triumphal entry, Jesus enters the temple and again He is provoked to anger. Outraged at the abuse and extortion, Jesus drives the money changers out a second time.

Then they came to Jerusalem. And He entered the temple and began to drive out those who were buying and selling in the temple, and overturned the tables of the money changers and the seats of those who were selling doves; and He would not permit anyone to carry merchandise through the temple.

MARK 11:15-16 NIV

The King James Version translates that He forbade them "to carry any vessel through the temple." Not just "any vessel" will qualify to serve in God's house.

Be clean, you who bear the vessels of the Lord.

ISAIAH 52:11B NKJV

The deeper message is that we are God's temple, and the Holy Spirit has chosen to live within us. He is God's supernatural glory living in His people on Earth today.

Do you not know that your bodies are temples of the Holy Spirit, who is in you, whom you have received from God? You are not your own...

1 Corinthians 6:19 NIV

Chapter 13

POWER ON
LIVING BY CONVICTION

CONVICTION

1. A fixed or firm belief

2. The act of convicting someone, as in a court of law; a declaration that a person is guilty of an offense.

> *"But I tell you the truth, it is to your advantage that I go away; for if I do not go away, the Helper will not come to you; but if I go, I will send Him to you. And He, when He comes, will convict the world concerning sin and righteousness and judgment..."*
>
> JOHN 16:7-8 NIV

The word conviction comes from the Latin *convictionem*, meaning the mental state of being convinced or the firm belief held as proven. The Greek word *elegchó* Jesus used in this verse carries meanings including convict, reprove, refute, to reprehend severely, chide, admonish, reprove, to chasten, or punish. No one enjoys chastisement but we're reminded that if we are not disciplined, we are not truly God's children (Hebrews 12:5; Job 5:17).

HELPS Word Studies provides another meaning in line with the first definition above: "to convince with solid, compelling evidence."

Conviction's work is two-fold, as explained by *Jamieson-Faucett-Brown's Commentary*: "But convict or convince is the thing intended; and as the one expresses the work of the Spirit on the unbelieving portion of mankind, and the other on the believing, it is better not to restrict it to either." (Biblehub.com, accessed May 7, 2018.) Said another way, sinners are *convicted as guilty* before God and those who yield to the Spirit's voice are *convinced of the Holy Spirit's power* to bring us into righteousness through Christ and to live before Him free of guilt. *Matthew Henry's Commentary* on this verse describes this aspect: "The coming of the Spirit would be of unspeakable advantage to the disciples. The Holy Spirit is our Guide, not only to show us the way, but to go with us by continued aids and influences. To be led into a truth is more than barely to know it; it is not only to have the notion of it in our heads, but the relish, and savour, and power of it in our hearts." (Ibid.) This is *living by conviction*, in the supernatural power of the Spirit within.

> *However, I am telling you nothing but the truth when I say it is profitable (good, expedient, advantageous) for you that I go away. Because if I do not go away, the Comforter (Counselor, Helper, Advocate, Intercessor, Strengthener, Standby) will not come to you [into close fellowship with you]; but if I go away, I will send Him to you [to be in close fellowship with you]. And when He comes, He will convict and convince the world and bring demonstration to it about sin and about righteousness (uprightness of heart and right standing with God)...*
>
> John 16:7-8 AMPC

God is not a guilt-monger. Conviction is the impression that produces a sense of guilt, but it's a "good guilt." This impression is not for destruction but for correction and perfection.

Correction is a key component of direction. When my kids were learning to drive, I would instruct them to drive straight on the road. Have you ever held the steering wheel firmly and driven straight? Not a good idea. To drive correctly you must continually make corrections. We have been given a clear path to eternity through Christ, but it must be often corrected.

Conviction helps to set us apart from the world we live in. Holiness in some groups within the modern "Pentecostal movement" seem more concerned with cosmetics, accessories, and dress codes. Although I do believe that God has ordained holiness for our lives, awareness of this comes through prayer and relationship with Christ. Holiness is not the way to Christ; Christ is the way to holiness.

Pain Management

Obviously, no one enjoys pain, but pain is good, really good. Pain is a necessary part of the human body staying healthy. Pain directs our awareness to the particular area that needs attention. Our pain response is a sophisticated relay system from our body to our brain. Pain is for your protection. If the brain registers pain, we alter the activity we are engaged in or we look for help.

> *There are two types of painful change: the pain of change or the pain of never changing.*

Conviction is similar to pain. Conviction doesn't necessarily feel good, but it points out what is potentially bad. Conviction warns and signals us to a problem area that must be corrected. Conviction calls for change. There are two types of painful change: the pain of change or the pain of never changing.

Pain Blockers

Medical breakthroughs have been successful in blocking chronic pain to certain regions of the body. These nerve blocks are medications that have been injected to block pain from specific groups of nerves (plexus or ganglion). This is a beneficial breakthrough in modern medicine.

The carnal man has always tried to cover or mask his own depravity. Like the nerve block, man will do anything to escape his self-inflicted pain. Sin is painful. Some resort to substance abuse, while others flee to perversion or other vices, but all find themselves wounded beyond repair except for the grace of God.

Good understanding giveth favour: but the way of transgressors is hard.

Proverbs 13:15 KJV

Holy Spirit conviction is the needful antidote to guide us back into right standing with God. The Holy Spirit will never allow you to feel good about your sin. If you do, it's a spirit but not the Holy Spirit. The Holy Spirit brings reproof for sin. He identifies sin so that it will be evicted, not coddled or coped with.

Our generation has been extremely gentle on iniquity. Unwilling to expose and evict, we have made peace with much evil. We think that we have evolved, and these liberal allowances accentuate our diversity, when they actually rob us of our destiny.

And the LORD said, "My Spirit will not remain with mankind forever, because they are corrupt."

Genesis 6:3a CSB

AGENT OF CHANGE

Conviction brings the desperate need for change out into the open. Conviction communicates to the soul the error of our way.

In "The Parable of the Lost Coin" (Luke 15:8-10), a woman loses one of ten coins. She immediately lights a lamp and sweeps her house until the coin is found. Immediately, this parable tells us two things about her house: It is dark and it is dirty.

Conviction not only communicates that something is wrong, it tells us that something is missing. We often want to make holiness complicated, while the Bible makes it simply clear: illuminate the darkness and eliminate the dirt. Whatever is missing in us (our house) can be fixed with a lamp and a broom.

> *Conviction not only communicates that something is wrong, it tells us that something is missing.*

The Holy Spirit has always had a sweeping effect towards cleanliness. Jesus promised the Holy Spirit would guide us in to all truth. Just like the example of the lost coin, the Spirit will bring things to remembrance. He will illuminate false belief and false motive. He convicts us of the "dirt" in our lives.

The Holy Spirit then guides us into change. Not for a moment or a day but real change. The kind of change that breaks the familiar patterns we've fallen prey to: the addictions, the cycles, the mindsets. Through the Spirit's illumination, we see more clearly so we can adjust more rapidly.

"If you always do, what you've always done, you will always get what you have always gotten."

HENRY FORD, FOUNDER OF THE FORD MOTOR COMPANY

UNCONTESTED IMMORALITY

The modern church era of "seeker sensitivity" will be responsible for countless souls unprepared and headed for eternal judgment. Those who have perpetuated this "don't ask, don't tell" ignorance will no doubt pay a heavy price for the souls that should have been redeemed through truth, rather than lost through empty, lifeless words offering false comfort.

Of course, the argument is "love." The seeker-sensitive church boasts of a greater love for the wayward while issuing license for acceptance of sin. This is deception through false hope. This is also false love and a faulty argument. If knowing full well that someone's actions are damnable, yet you refuse to speak up, you will never convince me that you love them. I am more likely to be convinced that you hate them if you know the devastating consequences of their actions and remain silent.

> Sometimes I feel like a dinosaur, but I would rather offend someone into eternal life than to encourage someone into eternal death.

There is a high demand for ministers to encourage only and never to offend. Sometimes I feel like a dinosaur, but I would rather offend someone into eternal life than to encourage someone into eternal death. Conviction of the Holy Spirit is what draws men to Christ.

THE PAINFUL PRICE FOR RELEVANCE

Many have sought for relevance at the expense of righteousness. Our loyalties have been swayed as we seek the approval of men rather than the approval of God. We can either be accepted by sinners and rejected by God or accepted by God and rejected by sinners.

Jesus knew how to be a friend of sinners while simultaneously restoring them. As the Spirit-led prototype, Jesus could convict of sin while convincing towards righteousness (right standing with God).

You can't win a cannibal by eating like one. God has always set a standard, and the Holy Spirit is the enforcer of that standard.

GOOD WITHOUT GOD, IS NOT GOOD AT ALL

It's good to do good, but doing "goodness" is not always doing "godliness." You can do good without God, but you cannot do God without good.

> *It's good to do good, but doing "goodness" is not always doing "godliness." You can do good without God, but you cannot do God without good.*

This generation feels justified because they have done more good for humanity than their predecessors. This is notable and opens many doors of opportunity, but that cannot be the only result.

The previous generation did us no favors by holding high standards without throwing out the ladder for the next guy. Many graduated from a "school of deliverance" but forgot where they came from and burned the schoolhouse down. Not all, but many of the previous generation were so concerned with "right living" that they had little time for "right doing."

So, the current generation finds things to make them feel better about themselves. They do good works, which is commendable, but they are lacking when it comes to holy living. It is common to crowd our lives with social causes and humanitarian efforts to soothe over our conviction from unrighteousness. We count on these good deeds to fill a deep void in our soul. Our works become the "little gods" that define our existence and temporarily bring relief from the emptiness. The worst form of "badness" is human goodness when it becomes the substitute for a relationship with the Redeemer.

So You Want to Feel Better

I once had a visitor to my church who had the audacity to tell me, "I would rather go to a church that makes me feel better about myself." I understood that it was a jab on his way out, but I still didn't know what had offended him. His comments have always rung in my ears; I don't know why he needed to feel better about himself. When we experience God and His grace, we don't feel better about ourselves, we feel better about our Savior.

Conviction points us to the remedy, not self-righteousness. We have never pulled ourselves up by our own proverbial bootstraps. We are not self-reliant or self-sustaining — we need a Savior.

There are movements under the guise of Christianity that prey upon the sinner and exploit the lost by going to great lengths and taking liberties to make them feel better about themselves. There are churches, especially in our western hemisphere, which will sanction anything except holiness. After all, you have to draw the line somewhere. Jude called these church leaders "clouds without water." (Jude 1:12)

Conviction vs. Condemnation

> *"If anyone hears my words and doesn't keep them, I don't condemn him, because I didn't come to condemn the world, but to save it. The one who rejects me and doesn't receive my words has something to judge him: The word that I've spoken will judge him on the last day..."*
>
> JOHN 12:47-48 ISV

The goal of conviction is not to make you feel bad, but to help you do good. Conviction is a gift from God. Condemnation is an assault from Satan.

The Voice of Conviction Says:
You've done wrong, just do right
You made a mistake
You've failed
There is a solution

The Voice of Condemnation Says:
You've done wrong, you can never do right
You are a mistake
You are a failure
You are the problem

For God did not send his Son into the world to condemn the world, but to save the world through him.

JOHN 3:17 NIV

The Lord delights in showing mercy. In fact, He longs to be gracious to us.

Who is a God like you, who pardons sin and forgives the transgression of the remnant of his inheritance? You do not stay angry forever but delight to show mercy.

MICAH 7:18 NIV

Accusation works through the voice of condemnation. Conviction draws us to God, while condemnation separates us from God. Conviction originates from the Holy Spirit, while condemnation comes from Satan, the accuser.

Conviction is specific, while condemnation is general. Conviction's focus is on the sin, while condemnation's focus is on the individual as a sinner.

Condemnation keeps long accounts, never allowing us freedom from past transgression. Blame and shame become the staple diet of those bound by condemnation. Condemnation is quick to find the problem but slow to search for the solution. If we have sinned, we ask for forgiveness. We declare with renewed hope and assurance, "I did it, but I'm not it."

According to 1 John 2:1, even if we sin, we have an advocate with God. We have an attorney (Jesus Christ, Esq.) at work, taking our case and restoring our standing with the Father, while the Holy Spirit confirms we are the sons of God.

Therefore, there is now no condemnation for those who are in Christ Jesus…

ROMANS 8:1 NIV

Let me reiterate what the Bible says: no condemnation, absolutely no condemnation. When we stand in this knowledge we disarm Satan of his tyrannous assault. Satan's attack is suspended and disabled.

In Paul's passage on spiritual warfare found in Ephesians 6:10-18, the word "wrestle" appears once while the word "stand" appears four times. We are not fighting *for* victory, we are fighting *from* victory. We stand fully aware that we are forgiven and that condemnation has no control over our life. We stand upon God's Word. We stand in the power of His might, not our own. And having done all to stand, well, we just stand!

God reminds you of who you are; Satan reminds you of who you were. Satan loves to dwell on the old you, but God is determined to promote the new you, the one He calls "a new creation."

My friend Ricardo said, "Satan knows your name, but calls you by your sin; God knows your sin, but calls you by your name." We have been justified freely (Romans 3:24).

OVERCORRECTION

While learning to drive, my cousin Stacey momentarily drifted off the road. Alarmed, he rapidly jerked the steering wheel back. Before he knew it, his car was flipping. We must always be aware that there is a ditch on both sides of the road.

It is possible to overcorrect a wrong. We should never be casual or flippant about sin, but we must realize there is help. Safely, we must realign and readjust our lives to what God intends for us to be. Life is full of adjustments. The Holy Spirit, through an internal witness of our spirit, continually monitors and warns us to be on guard. The Spirit teaches us to correct without overcorrection. This gift of grace is a divine enablement to operate freely without restriction, while trusting in God's provision.

"You can stand so straight; you fall over backwards."

Doug Morgan

SET YOUR HOUSE IN ORDER

My father died October 2, 1995. He was a wonderful pastor and an incredible dad. He was renowned for his wisdom and for being a pastor to pastors.

"God buries His workmen, but the work goes on."

Charles Wesley, carved on a monument commemorating the life and death of John Wesley at Westminster Abby

The steps of a good man are ordered by the Lord, and He delights in his way.

Psalms 37:23 NKJV

My dad was a renaissance man. His hands were in everything. If he couldn't fix it, he would take it apart then fix it. A mechanic, a carpenter, a musician, a disciplined scholar, a teacher, a lover of God's Word. He built two of the homes I grew up in. When I think of his skill set, I'm amazed because he came from an impoverished family. He just had a desire to work and was not afraid to learn. My youngest brother shares many of these same qualities.

My father taught me how to clear my mind of "can't." He was an assertive leader but never pushy. He always said, "No one will stop you if you look like you know where you're going."

Jesus said, "To whom much is given, much is required" (Luke 12:48). Spiderman rephrased this by saying, "With great power comes great responsibility."

My dad died at the young age of 57. For the last decade of his life, he had been privately dealing with illness. At 6'3' and 240 pounds, it was difficult to see him wean down to 160 pounds. He was skin and bones but full of conviction and Holy Ghost anointing. He grew a beard because so many commented on his thinning face. Before long, he had the appearance of a biblical character right out of the Old Testament. I am so proud of him; I want to be like him. I have good roots. One of my greatest desires is that the fruit reflects its roots.

The boundary lines have fallen in pleasant places for me; truly, I have a beautiful heritage.

PSALMS 16:6 ISV

Dad's illness took its toll on him physically. From a distance, his suit looked like it was on a hanger as he passionately shared the gospel, compelling the lost to experience salvation. He gave everything to God, everything.

Let me take you back for a moment. My father was born in a farmhouse in the foothills of the Blue Ridge Mountains. He had no birth certificate. A neighbor lady helped in the delivery, and that was that.

As a farm boy, my father was unusually tall and lanky. He was well respected in his farm community. I personally know this because decades later he would buy a forty-acre farm in those same foothills. Many people never left the mountain, and all seemed to be familiar with Doug. He was loved in his small, rural community. As a young man, he and some other rambunctious boys from the hills would sometimes blow off some steam and get drunk on the weekends.

My dad was juxtaposed between two lifestyles. My grandmother Carrie loved the Lord, but for many years, my grandfather had nothing to do with God. Carrie always had a family Bible open on the dining room table. My dad said it scared him, so he tried to avoid it as he walked around the outskirts of the living room in the old farmhouse. However, something always captivated him about that book. Interestingly, in a Bible he gave me, he had handwritten, "Sin will keep you from this book, and this book will keep you from sin."

One wild night, which he really didn't remember (or didn't really want to remember), he and his friends ended up in the county dump. (That much, he remembered.) They didn't have landfills in that day, just heaps of trash pushed and piled up in rows. This was a commentary on his life; he thought, "I have wasted my life and I'm good for nothing."

As he awakened from an inebriated state, he crawled out of the cramped car filled with young, restless men. Each man had potential,

Supernatural Power on Earth

> You can never cross the ocean if you refuse to lose sight of the shoreline.

but none had purpose. That was the night he resigned to himself; that was the night he surrendered his will. That night changed the trajectory of his life. He didn't know how to be saved, but he was definitely under conviction. He walked away — literally, he crawled out and walked away. You can never cross the ocean if you refuse to lose sight of the shoreline.

You can call this a change of heart, a fresh start, or regret, but I think this was the pathway to salvation. When it comes to true salvation, ignorance does not penalize you from God's grace. Don't let anyone tell you differently. Although he had not learned how to officially "repent," he was sorry. In biblical terms, this is called contrition, or "godly sorrow." That is what touches the heart of God, not a choreographed string of words. Phrases like "Remember me when you come into your Kingdom" actually unlock the heavens.

"The two most important days in your life are the day you are born and the day you find out why."

COMMONLY ATTRIBUTED TO MARK TWAIN

My father still had addictions in his life, but something (Someone) was stirring a response that he could not resist. Like the prophet Amos, "The Lord took him."

My great uncle Willie Matt, was a Pentecostal preacher. He influenced my dad to go to Lee College. Lee College was a school that taught the Bible; there was no other academic training available, Bible only, for the purpose of preaching the gospel.

The Distance between Calling and Commission

Long and short of it, my grandmother made my dad two bag lunches, and with his life savings of $1.13, off he went. Unbelievably determined and inadequately prepared, he walked to the highway and began to hitchhike towards a destination three states to the north. No high school transcript, no birth certificate, no money, no fear.

I know this sounds far-fetched, but it really happened. Holy Spirit conviction is profoundly perceived in the call of God on a life.

Ecclesiastes 3:11 says, "God has placed eternity in our hearts." If that is true, then our heart holds a memory of our future. When we are dealing with disappointment, our heart may actually be letting us know that we are off course from the picture it holds of our destiny. Are you saying, "My heart is clairvoyant?" No, I'm just saying you have an innate feeling that can't be described. Some call this a "knowing." It's a discerning spirit that prevents you from drifting too far if you will only listen. We know this to be the voice of the Holy Spirit, God's supernatural power on Earth.

> When we are dealing with disappointment, our heart may actually be letting us know that we are off course from the picture it holds of our destiny.

Although my dad did not have a relationship with God, He was still speaking to him through the conviction of the Holy Spirit. In fact, I would venture to say that when he lifted his thumb on a deserted back road, he was hastening to the compelling call of God. It is His grace that can deposit a revelation of God, even before a relationship has been established.

The rest is nothing less than miraculous. Smoking a cigarette on the doorstep of this Bible school, he was declined acceptance with

Supernatural Power on Earth

no transcript, no money, and no true identity. Providentially, he was embraced by a faculty member that saw potential. Dad bartered his way into college, covering his tuition by working in the school cafeteria.

In a campus chapel service, he "properly" confessed his sins. This is hard to believe or even relate to for those, like myself, that grew up blessed with opportunity. Dad would say, "With God nothing is impossible!"

At the age of 29, he would be preaching on a Friday night at the General Assembly, the most coveted platform in his denomination. This awkwardly courageous, unconventional, young man will preach at this international summit, a place usually reserved for the qualified, seasoned veteran. Promotion does not come from the east or the west, promotion comes from God. Man can't choose who God will use!

THE CLOSING CHAPTER

This brings me to the closing chapter of my father's life. He is worn out; at 57 years old he appears much older. He physically struggles to make it out of bed, but he gets up and gets ready. This will be the last Sunday God will require of this poor country boy that made it good. He walks to the church, a multi-million-dollar campus that God has allowed him to build.

Fast-forward to the message, this will be his final act of public service to his King. The text reads as follows:

In those days was Hezekiah sick unto death. And Isaiah the prophet the son of Amoz came unto him, and said unto him, Thus saith the LORD, Set thine house in order: for thou shalt die, and not live.

Isaiah 38:1 KJV

He preaches with vigor and passion. He pours out his heart; where he finds the strength only God knows. The word is strong and powerful. Conviction resonates throughout the attentive congregation. "Set your house in order. Set your house in order!"

As he delivers his final closing statements, he is completely spent! He has left it all on the field! There's nothing left. The ushers notice he's reeling, losing his balance. Like guardian angels, they run to his side. They carry him from the pulpit like a child; the duty-bound men carry him all the way home. If that seems overdramatic, I guess it was, unless you knew the rest of the story. They laid him on a reclining chair, and there he stayed until God took him home.

"His master replied, 'Well done, good and faithful servant! You have been faithful with a few things; I will put you in charge of many things. Come and share your master's happiness!'"

MATTHEW 25:23 NIV

The Holy Spirit guides us and teaches us how to live responsibly before God and with man. A fulfilled life is the consequence of adopting responsibility. The result is a life of intentionality rather than regret. The Holy Spirit says to you and to me, "Set your house in order. Set your house in order!"

"He is no fool to give what he cannot keep, to gain what he cannot lose."

JIM ELLIOT, *THE JOURNALS OF JIM ELLIOT*,
EDITED BY ELISABETH ELLIOTT, BAKER BOOKS, 2002

Chapter 14

POWER ON
APPLICATION

RECOGNIZE WHAT'S IN YOU

Adam Rainer was born in Graz, Austria. Adam had a rare medical history. You see, he was born as a dwarf, but in the course of his lifetime he eventually grew into a giant. He is the only documented dwarf giant recorded in history.

At age 19, he was 4'8" and rejected from the military because of his abnormally small size. Over the next decade, he grew to a shocking 7'1," with a size 20 shoe. At death, he measured 7'8." He never quit growing! (Source: *TheBusinessInsider.com*, Dr. Lindsey Fitzharris, *The Chirurgeon's Apprentice*, January 22, 2015. Accessed May 15, 2018.)

This is a bazaar story, but inside each of us are a pygmy and a powerhouse. We are equipped with such great potential but many never tap in to it although it's there, lying dormant and waiting to be activated.

Now to him who is able to do immeasurably more than all we ask or imagine, according to his power that is at work within us...

EPHESIANS 3:20 NIV

Supernatural Power on Earth

Knowing there is potential changes nothing; waking up the potential changes everything. Knowledge without application is just information. Information without application is like having a bank account with no way to access the money—worthless!

So the question is, "Would you rather have information or transformation?" You've made it to the back of this book, which is evidence of your desire to experience the Holy Spirit to His fullest.

BORN OF THE SPIRIT

Let's begin with salvation. Salvation is the will of God and the initial step in experiencing His supernatural presence. It is the starting place — it was never meant to be the resting place. This is where we begin our wonderful journey with the Lord.

First, we repent. We confess our sins to God, understanding He stands ready to forgive because of Jesus' substitutionary sacrifice. So, we come clean, we confess our sin. We own it for a moment, then we move on.

> *But what does it say? "The word is near you, in your mouth and in your heart" (that is, the word of faith which we preach): that if you confess with your mouth the Lord Jesus and believe in your heart that God has raised Him from the dead, you will be saved. For with the heart one believes unto righteousness, and with the mouth confession is made unto salvation.*
>
> ROMANS 10:8-10 NKJV

> *Therefore, there is now no condemnation for those who are in Christ Jesus, because through Christ Jesus the law of the Spirit who gives life has set you free from the law of sin and death.*
>
> ROMANS 8:1-2 NIV

No condemnation—that's God's promise to us. Amazing! We may have *done it* (sin) but *we* are *not it!* Every label that falsely ties you to it is a lie. We become a new creation. Our slate has been wiped clean. "Forgiven of much? Loved much." That's our Father's guarantee.

But to as many as did receive and welcome Him, He gave the authority (power, privilege, right) to become the children of God, that is, to those who believe in (adhere to, trust in, and rely on) His name - Who owe their birth neither to bloods nor to the will of the flesh [that of physical impulse] nor to the will of man [that of a natural father], but to God. [They are born of God!]

JOHN 1:12-13 AMPC

We now have trust and confidence in His faithfulness rather than live in doubt or regret because of our past unfaithfulness. There is freedom to live, freedom to grow, and it may sound controversial, but there is even freedom to fall, as long as we fall forward.

You are now born of the Spirit. Make no mistake about it; you have the Holy Spirit living on the inside of you. Greater is He that is in you, than he that would condemn you (1 John 4:4). God's grace has sanctioned your success. You are now born again.

Jesus answered, "Very truly I tell you, no one can enter the kingdom of God unless they are born of water and the Spirit. Flesh gives birth to flesh, but the Spirit gives birth to spirit. You should not be surprised at my saying, 'You must be born again.' The wind blows wherever it pleases. You hear its sound, but you

cannot tell where it comes from or where it is going. So it is with everyone born of the Spirit."

JOHN 3:5-8 NIV

If you are born twice, you will only die once. If you are only born once, you will die twice: once at the death of this earthly life and the second time at the eternal death to come. Being born again is synonymous to being born of the Spirit. Now, on to the next level for there is so much more. Times of refreshing!

Repent, then, and turn to God, so that your sins may be wiped out, that times of refreshing may come from the Lord

ACTS 3:19 NIV

His power works within us. The Holy Spirit is more than *on* us, He is also *in* us. This is why we are given the mandate to stir up this gift that's on the inside of us.

The Holy Spirit is mentioned 261 times in the New Testament alone. He is of the utmost importance. Don't attempt to do life utilizing only two-thirds of the Godhead. The Spirit desires to be present and active in your daily walk on Earth. He wants your consecration; He wants your communication; we need His cooperation.

> More than arrogant, it would be tragic to neglect God's unfathomable gift of Himself, the Holy Spirit.

Since you were saved, He has been on standby, waiting for you. So right now, I would like to invite you to welcome the Holy Spirit into your life. It is possible to receive a gift and never unwrap it.

Application

That would be more than arrogant, it would be tragic to neglect God's unfathomable gift of Himself, the Holy Spirit.

BAPTISM OF THE SPIRIT

At salvation you were born of the Spirit, now you are ready for the baptism of the Spirit. The Spirit will lead you into the deeper presence of God. This is what Jesus called "the promise of the Father," for which His people had waited thousands of years. He's now here and waiting for you to simply believe, desire, and receive! Ask Jesus to open your mind to understand so you will be enrobed with His supernatural power from Heaven.

> *Then he opened their minds so they could understand the Scriptures. He told them, "This is what is written: The Messiah will suffer and rise from the dead on the third day, and repentance for the forgiveness of sins will be preached in his name to all nations, beginning at Jerusalem. You are witnesses of these things. I am going to send you what my Father has promised; but stay in the city until you have been clothed with power from on high."*
>
> LUKE 24:45-49 NIV

He'd told them that He would leave and they would be His witnesses, but He also told them He wouldn't leave them alone as orphans (John 14:16-18). In fact, He said it was actually advantageous for Him to leave so that the Promised One could come.

> *However, I am telling you nothing but the truth when I say it is profitable (good, expedient, advantageous) for you that I go*

away. Because if I do not go away, the Comforter (Counselor, Helper, Advocate, Intercessor, Strengthener, Standby) will not come to you [into close fellowship with you]; but if I go away, I will send Him to you [to be in close fellowship with you].

JOHN 16:6-7 AMPC

It's hard to imagine that anything would be more advantageous than having Jesus personally present with you! Nevertheless, it's true—He has sent the Holy Spirit to empower and equip every believer who seeks Him. Jesus is the Baptizer in the Holy Spirit—He sends the Spirit to you from the Father.

But when the Comforter (Counselor, Helper, Advocate, Intercessor, Strengthener, Standby) comes, Whom I will send to you from the Father, the Spirit of Truth Who comes (proceeds) from the Father, He [Himself] will testify regarding Me.

JOHN 15:26 AMPC

When He appeared to them after resurrection, Jesus told His followers not to leave the city until the promise of the Holy Spirit was given to them. They couldn't live the powerful life God desires without His supernatural ability (and neither can we). They were to wait for the fulfillment of the Feast of Pentecost, when the rushing wind and flaming tongues of fire appeared on every believer who'd sought Him. (Read Acts 2.)

Read the words of Luke, who again uses the phrase "baptized with the Holy Spirit." See how the priority is stressed and that this baptism is distinct from water baptism.

After his suffering, he presented himself to them and gave many convincing proofs that he was alive. He appeared to them over a period of forty days and spoke about the kingdom of God. On one occasion, while he was eating with them, he gave them this command: "Do not leave Jerusalem, but wait for the gift my Father promised, which you have heard me speak about. For John baptized with water, but in a few days you will be baptized with the Holy Spirit."

Acts 1:2-5 NIV

This is consistent with the apostle Paul's impartation of the Holy Spirit to the Ephesian believers. They had already believed and been baptized in water, followed by baptism in the Holy Spirit:

While Apollos was at Corinth, Paul took the road through the interior and arrived at Ephesus. There he found some disciples and asked them, "Did you receive the Holy Spirit when you believed?" They answered, "No, we have not even heard that there is a Holy Spirit." So Paul asked, "Then what baptism did you receive?" "John's baptism," they replied. Paul said, "John's baptism was a baptism of repentance. He told the people to believe in the one coming after him, that is, in Jesus." On hearing this, they were baptized in the name of the Lord Jesus. When Paul placed his hands on them, the Holy Spirit came on them, and they spoke in tongues and prophesied.

Acts 19:1-6 NIV

Note that when "the Holy Spirit came on them they spoke in tongues and prophesied." Speaking in tongues is an outward evidence of baptism into the Spirit. (For more detail and scriptures on this, refer to Chapter 9, the section "Manifestation of Baptism in the Holy Spirit.") Speaking in tongues is the Holy Spirit inspiring within you the highest form of communication with God. Immediate and long-term benefits include peace, power, and divine direction.

But you, beloved, building yourselves up on your most holy faith, praying in the Holy Spirit...

JUDE 20 NIV

I cannot predict who will or who won't speak in tongues. I believe that this is a gift from God that all believers can experience, not just a select few. (Refer to Chapter 9, "Tongues as a Prayer Language.")

LIFE-CHANGING POWER

When the Holy Spirit's presence and power floods a believer, the results are truly life-changing. As mentioned before, the life of the apostle Peter is a great example. He swore he'd never forsake the Lord, only to be fearful of a servant-girl who said she'd seen him with Jesus. Out of fear, he actually cursed and denied Him three times. After he was baptized in the Holy Spirit, he was transformed—he no longer feared man (or woman) and spoke powerfully, regardless of the consequences.

The Spirit continues to transform believers by His supernatural power. He is the game-changer for those who've struggled helplessly with sin and addictions—they find the Spirit gives strength to overcome (Romans 7:14-25). Those with anger or other deeply entrenched character flaws find the fruit of the Spirit (love, patience, etc.) comes (super)naturally as His character is formed in them (Galatians 5:16-25).

Believers who once felt powerless in their walk with God, feeling there must be more and searching for strength to do His will, find the needed joy and power (Colossians 1:9-14). Those who grieve at the condition of the world's sick, poor, and hopeless find the gifts of the Spirit are available to bring solutions for every human condition.

> *The Spirit is not one-size-fits-all. He clothes each believer in a spiritual garment exactly suited to their personal struggles, aptitudes, giftings, and calling.*

An amazing thing about this wonderful gift is that it's not one-size-fits-all. He clothes each believer in a spiritual garment exactly suited to their personal struggles, aptitudes, giftings, and calling—a perfect fit! The Holy Spirit knows our weaknesses, struggles, and fears—as said before, He works to change you from the inside out. Your *desires* will change as He writes God's ways and will on your heart. You will have the *power to live and act differently* as He lives and works deeply and intimately *inside you.*

You show that you are a letter from Christ, the result of our ministry, written not with ink but with the Spirit of the living God, not on tablets of stone but on tablets of human hearts.

2 CORINTHIANS 3:3 NIV

"This is the covenant I will make with them after that time, says the Lord. I will put my laws in their hearts, and I will write them on their minds."

HEBREWS 10:16 NIV

Seek, inquire of and for the Lord, and crave Him and His strength (His might and inflexibility to temptation); seek and require His face and His presence [continually] evermore. Who satisfies your mouth [your necessity and desire at your personal age and situation] with good so that your youth, renewed, is like the eagle's [strong, overcoming, soaring]!

Psalm 103:4-5 AMPC

You will not fail because the Holy Spirit's supernatural ability will transform and empower you to overcome every sin, addiction, personality flaw, sickness, and every other obstacle to your success—He is omnipotent and has promised to share his power with *you*!

I want to share four things that I believe will prepare you for this life-changing experience with God:

1. Repent
2. Ask
3. Surrender
4. Worship

REPENT

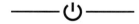

Peter replied, "Repent and be baptized, every one of you, in the name of Jesus Christ for the forgiveness of your sins. And you will receive the gift of the Holy Spirit.

Acts 2:38 NIV

Have you ever had a bad cell phone connection? Because you are having trouble hearing the other line, you may even get louder, which doesn't necessarily mean they can't hear you clearly. It's just a bad connection. Repentance clears the connection. Communication no longer has to be forced or awkward.

ASK

> *"So I say to you: Ask and it will be given to you; seek and you will find; knock and the door will be opened to you. For everyone who asks receives; the one who seeks finds; and to the one who knocks, the door will be opened."*
>
> LUKE 11:9-10 NIV

Asking is demonstration of intent. We always ask for what we want, either verbally, by posture, or by behavior. We let our intentions be known if it is important enough to us.

I suggest doing this alone. I could support this, but I would rather just reiterate that true intent is established in private. What happens in private is evidence of the genuine. Truth has a private address; lies love a crowd.

Get alone with God. Private prayers result in public power. This is not an audition; this is not role-play. This is you and God; this is beautiful. Don't allow any room for distractions. This is what God desires for you and you're ready. Now ask. He's been eagerly waiting on you. Ask to be ignited by His presence. You may need to ask more than once—don't be disappointed if you don't receive the first time. He *wants* to be sought after. In fact, in the language Jesus spoke the words last quoted, the verb tense means to *keep on* asking, *keep on* seeking, *keep on* knocking. Just don't give up—believe and it will be opened to you!

> *"So I say to you, ask and keep on asking, and it will be given to you; seek and keep on seeking, and you will find; knock and keep on knocking, and the door will be opened to you. For everyone who keeps on asking [persistently], receives; and he who keeps on*

seeking [persistently], finds; and to him who keeps on knocking [persistently], the door will be opened."

LUKE 11:9-101 AMP

SURRENDER

We become apprehensive at any thought of losing control—we all want control. So this part seems to be the most difficult. You can want control and want the Spirit, but you can't have them both. To receive the Spirit, you must surrender control. In order for His Kingdom to come, your kingdom must go. David said, "I have set the Lord always before me." God must be preeminent — He must be first in priority.

For some, unwillingness to yield to the Spirit is a sign that we don't trust God. We keep Him at arm's length. The strange thing is that we trust ourselves, and we know that we've let ourselves down repeatedly. For others, the inability to surrender is fear based. They may be afraid that another spirit may take control. This is a tactic of the enemy to prevent you from trusting God. Read the words of Jesus, Who promised that if we ask for something good (and the Holy Spirit is Good!), our Father will not give us something evil:

"Which of you fathers, if your son asks for a fish, will give him a snake instead? Or if he asks for an egg, will give him a scorpion? If you then, though you are evil, know how to give good gifts to your children, how much more will your Father in heaven give the Holy Spirit to those who ask him!"

LUKE 11:10-13 NIV

Trust the Spirit, believe that He wants the best for you, and that He will provide a safe place to land. In receiving, you are welcoming and inviting God's Holy Spirit to consume you totally.

You're not *bringing* a sacrifice, *you are* the sacrifice. All sacrifices were eventually burned with fire. We can desire His fire, even though we don't deserve His fire. Contend for the fire. It is promised that Jesus will baptize you with the Holy Spirit and with fire—let Him blaze within you!

> *It is promised that Jesus will baptize you with the Holy Spirit and with fire — let Him blaze within you!*

John answered them all, "I baptize you with water. But one who is more powerful than I will come, the straps of whose sandals I am not worthy to untie. He will baptize you with the Holy Spirit and fire.

LUKE 3:16 NIV

You can be loud, you can be soft, you can just be. The most important thing is not what you say but what you surrender. "All of me, take all of me." The Holy Spirit loves to be engaged. He especially loves your sincere pursuit. When we surrender, we are no longer running against the wind, but running with it! Go all in! Welcome Holy Spirit! Welcome Holy Spirit! I am Yours…

WORSHIP

Praise is progressive. Thanksgiving and gratitude create an atmosphere for the miraculous. I'm referring to the supernatural power of God on Earth. God inhabits praise.

There are many ways to worship: You may meditate and read the Word of God; you may sing hymns or the Psalms; you can listen to worship music. All of these are powerful ways to get into the presence of God.

Supernatural Power on Earth

Just as you would prepare for a first date with your future spouse, you prepare for something this important. You pray, you seek the Lord. You may get loud and demonstrative or soft and pliable.

I have found significant results in quiet — for me, being quiet is powerful. My world is loud; in the quiet, I focus and lean in to His presence profoundly. In letting your words be few, you allow the heart to speak. I often conserve my words, because words cannot do justice to His presence. I have a limited vocabulary. I am saying in my silence that when I open my mouth, I would like to be speaking in Your language rather than mine. Knowing the limits of my language allows me to focus on the sound of Heaven.

In the same way the Spirit also helps our weakness; for we do not know how to pray as we should, but the Spirit Himself intercedes for us with groanings too deep for words; and He who searches the hearts knows what the mind of the Spirit is, because He intercedes for the saints according to the will of God.

ROMANS 8:26-27 NIV

You don't know what you don't know. Profound, right? We need help from another world. This supernatural power has been promised to us, and God not only *does not* lie, He *cannot* lie! His Word is true! So when we don't know… trust the Spirit. Receive the Holy Spirit, the supernatural power of God on Earth!

"You will receive power when the Holy Spirit comes on you; and you will be my witnesses…to the ends of the earth."

ACTS 1:8 NIV